THE INTERACTIVE
HUMAN
BODY

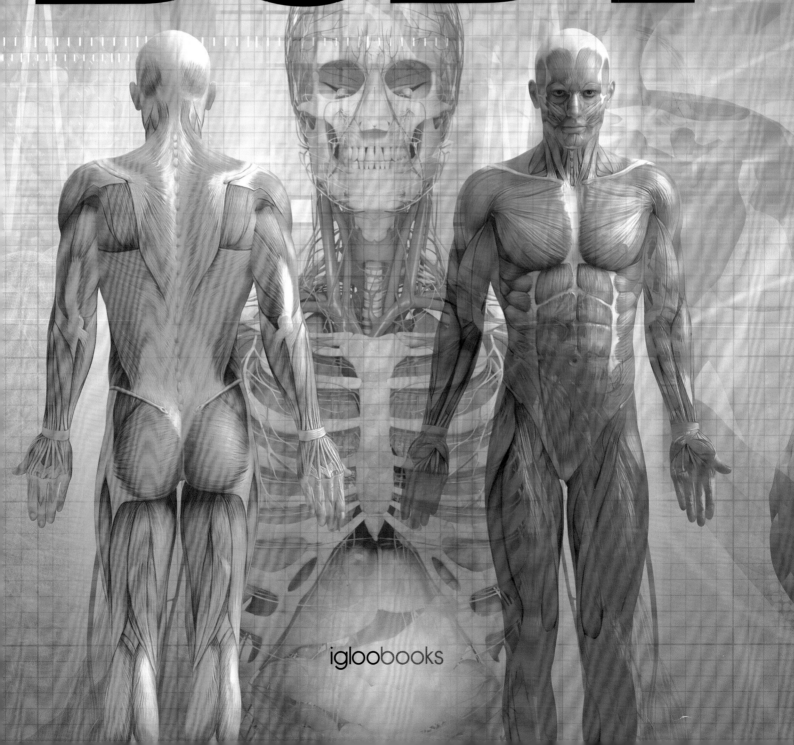

igloobooks

igloobooks

Published in 2013
by Igloo Books Ltd
Cottage Farm
Sywell
NN6 0BJ
www.igloobooks.com

SHE001 0713
2 4 6 8 10 9 7 5 3 1
ISBN 978-1-78197-544-2

Printed and manufactured in China

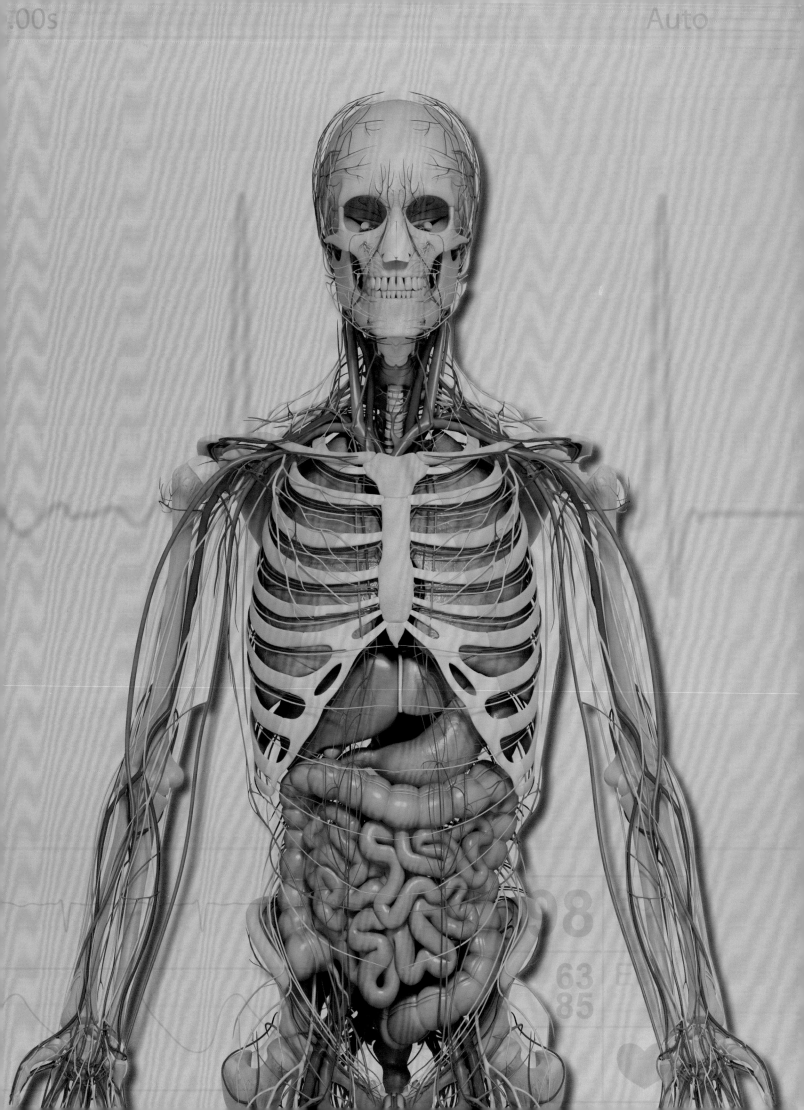

CONTENTS

Interactive Instructions

On your mobile, or tablet device, download the **FREE** Layar App.

Look out for the **SCAN ME** logo and scan the whole page.

Unlock, discover and enjoy the enhanced content.

For more details, visit: **www.igloobooks.com**

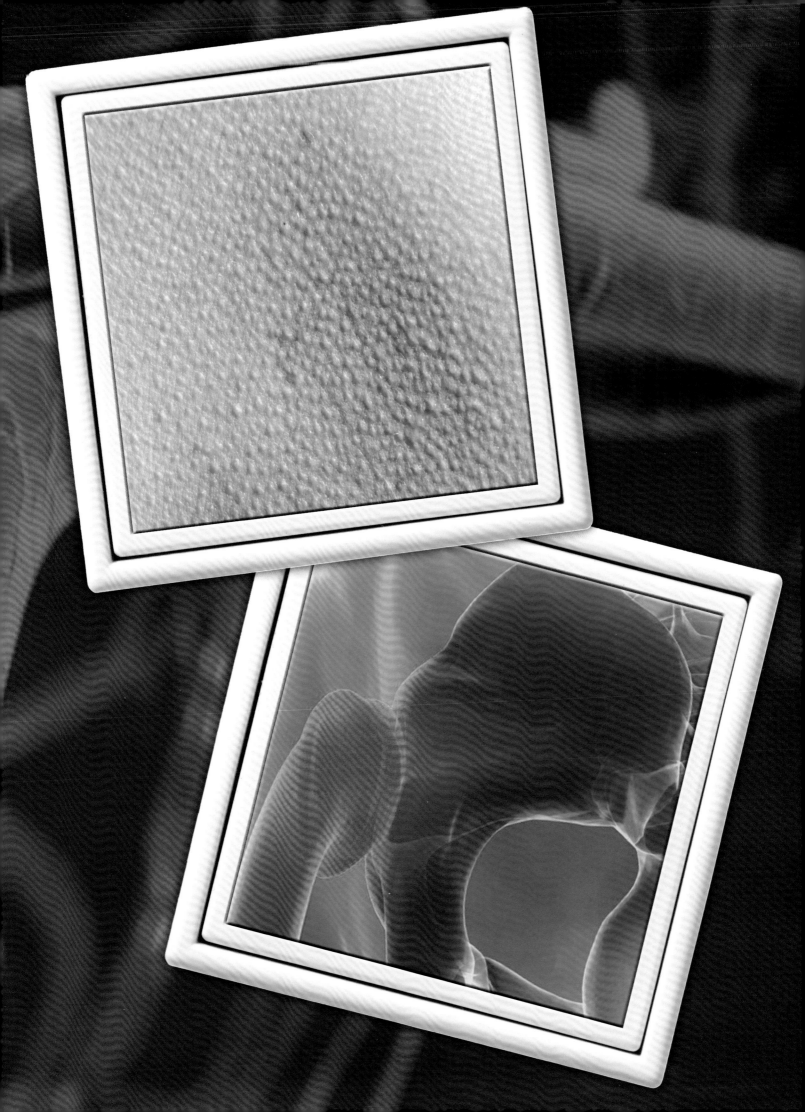

INTRODUCTION

The human body is an amazing piece of natural complex technology, made up of billions of tiny building blocks called cells. All of these cells do different jobs. Cells of the same type group together to form tissue. Cells and tissues are organized into larger body parts called organs and these organs form part of the essential systems that run our bodies. All of these cells, tissues, organs and systems are held together within an internal frame called the skeleton. The skeleton holds our bodies up and gives us our strength and shape and it also protects our internal organs and allows us to move. Finally, we have our muscles and skin, which cover the skeleton and hold everything together. These are very important because without them, our bones and organs would be hanging out all over the place!

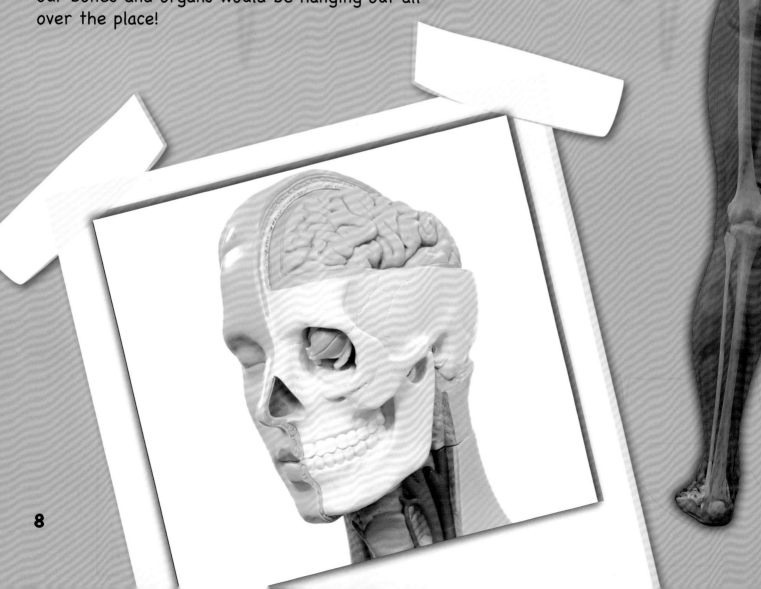

Every second of every day, our bodies are doing incredible things that we are not even aware of. These processes keep us alive, help us fight diseases and allow us to walk and talk and enjoy the world around us. If you take just five minutes to think of all the things you do in a day, from blinking your eyes to doing your homework, you realize how truly awesome our bodies are.

From head to toe, the human body can be divided into:

The head – which consists of the skull and face. Our skull houses the brain, the control room of our bodies. The face is specially designed to accommodate the eyes, mouth and nose, from where most of the information about our daily lives is collected.

The neck – this is the narrow part of the body which connects our head to our body.

The thorax, or chest – this is the part of the body which lies between the neck and the abdomen and contains two of the most vital organs of our body, the heart and the lungs.

The abdomen and pelvis – this is the area below the thorax and contains the organs that help us digest our food.

The upper limbs – each upper limb consists of shoulder, arm, forearm, hand and fingers.

The lower limbs – each lower limb consists of hip, thigh, leg, ankle, heel, foot and toes.

Our bodies come in many different shapes and sizes and, apart from identical twins, no two people are alike. Humans come with different skin colors, hair colors, and eye colors, as well as different shaped features such as our noses, mouths and ears. Some people are tall while others are short. But even though there is a great range of difference in our appearance, all our bodies contain the same parts. We all have 206 bones, 600 muscles and 22 internal organs.

There is still so much left to discover about the more complicated areas of our bodies. The human brain is one of the most complex organs on our planet. There are as many neurons in the brain as there are stars in the Milky Way galaxy so it is no surprise that, despite amazing recent advances in the science of the brain, we still find ourselves with so many questions yet unanswered about how our brains work. It is also true that there is still so much to discover about cells, DNA and genes and how to beat some of the nastier diseases our bodies can catch. We will help you to find out what we as humans already know.

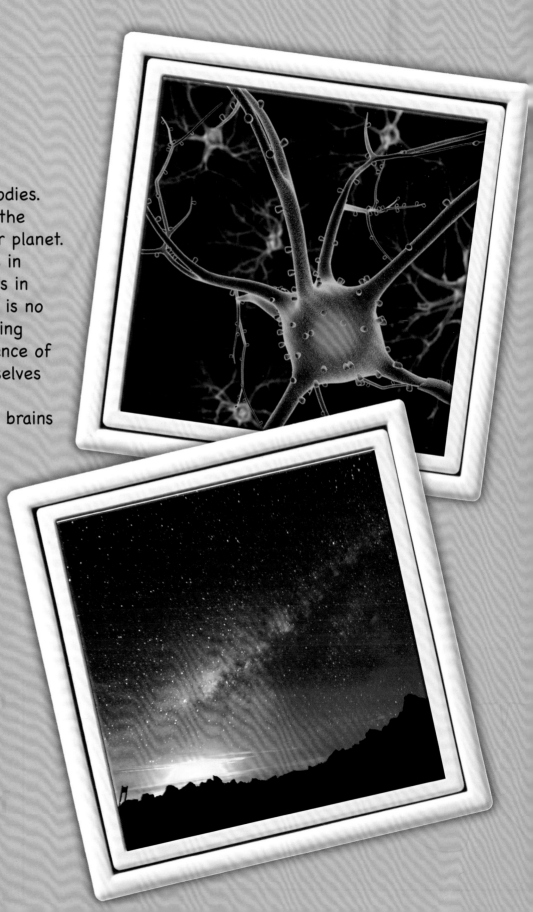

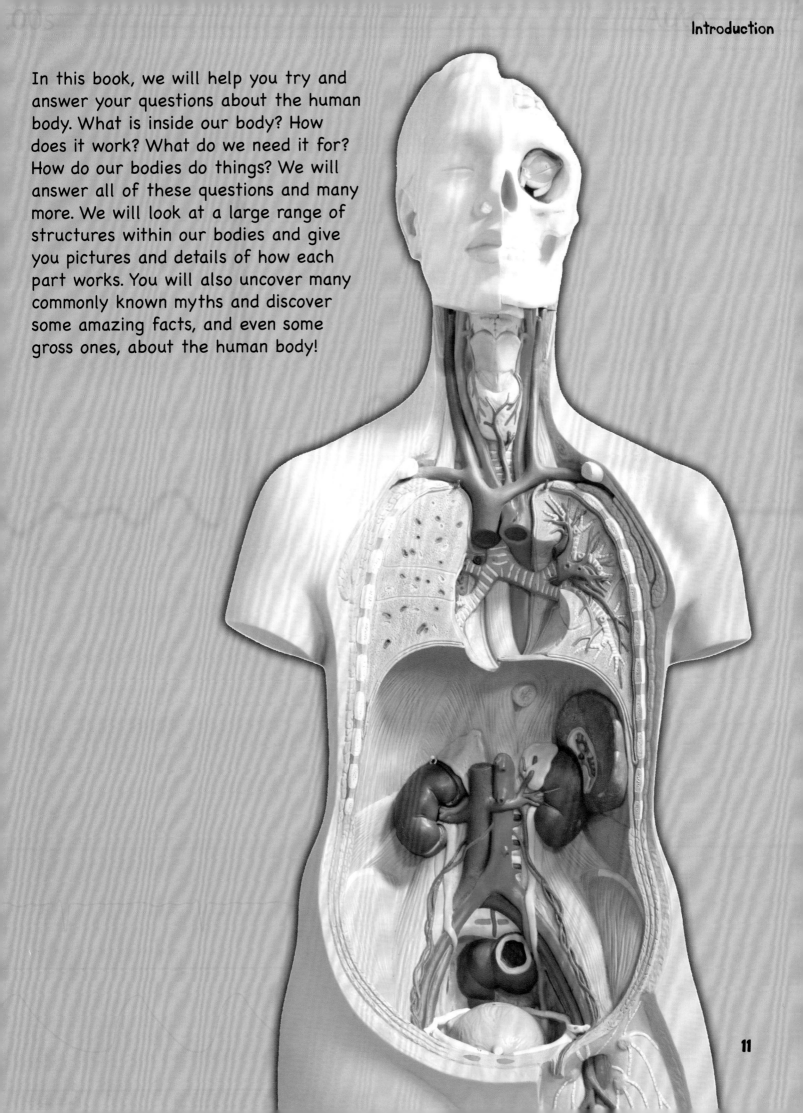

In this book, we will help you try and answer your questions about the human body. What is inside our body? How does it work? What do we need it for? How do our bodies do things? We will answer all of these questions and many more. We will look at a large range of structures within our bodies and give you pictures and details of how each part works. You will also uncover many commonly known myths and discover some amazing facts, and even some gross ones, about the human body!

THE SKULL

One of the most important and complex parts of the human skeleton is the skull. The skull is very important as it provides armored protection to one of the most vital human organs: the brain. However, only the upper dome-shaped part of the skull protects the brain. The lower part creates a background structure which gives each human their facial features. Human facial features are not biologically important but they do play an important role within our social environment; similar features – such as two eyes, one nose and one mouth – placed in roughly the same place on a face help humans to identify each other as the same species.

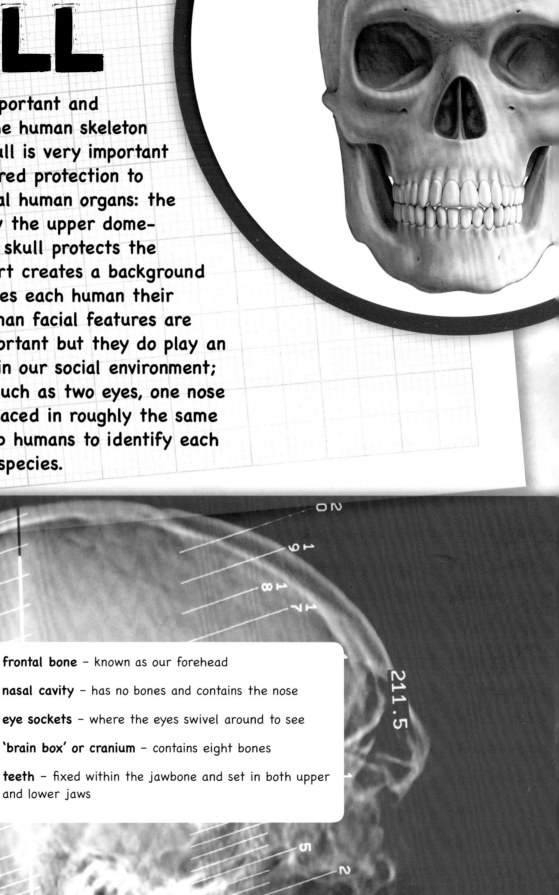

frontal bone – known as our forehead

nasal cavity – has no bones and contains the nose

eye sockets – where the eyes swivel around to see

'brain box' or cranium – contains eight bones

teeth – fixed within the jawbone and set in both upper and lower jaws

WOW - BRINGING THE DEAD ALIVE

The lower part of the skull plays such an important part in the basis of facial features that modern technology allows scientists to work out what a person's face would have looked like just by analyzing the skull and facial bones. This process is called facial reconstruction and is applied in many fields, including forensic science and archeology.

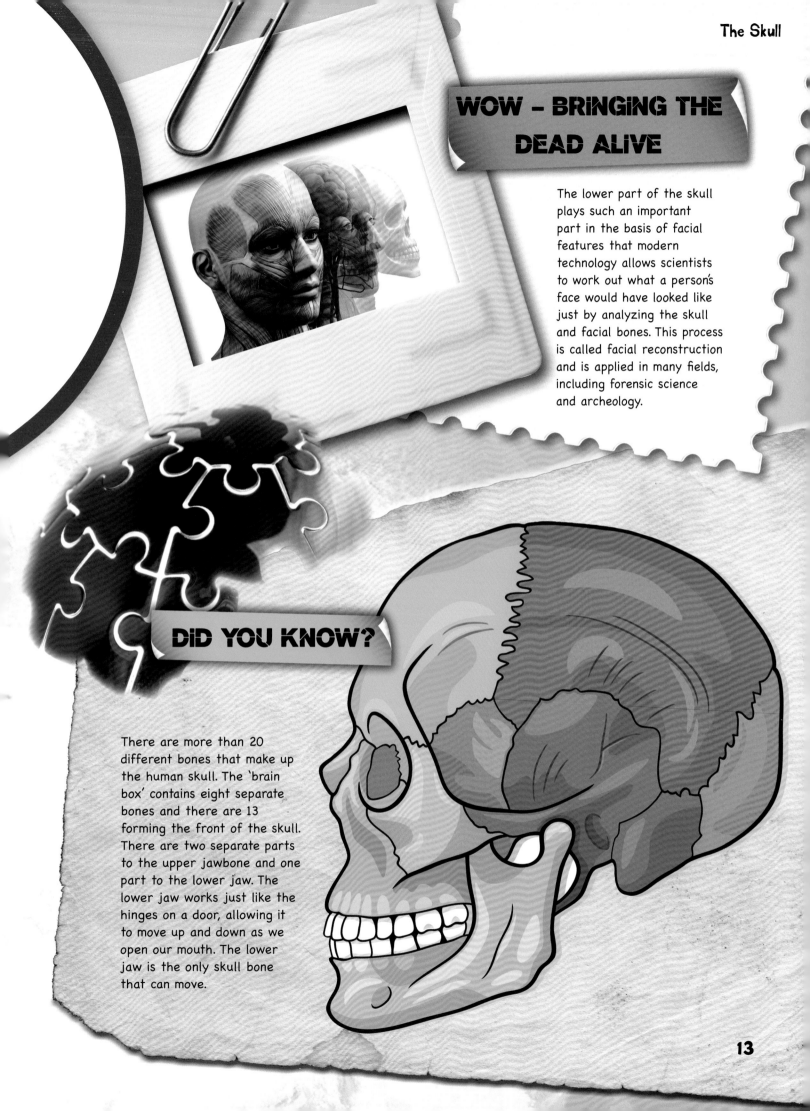

DID YOU KNOW?

There are more than 20 different bones that make up the human skull. The 'brain box' contains eight separate bones and there are 13 forming the front of the skull. There are two separate parts to the upper jawbone and one part to the lower jaw. The lower jaw works just like the hinges on a door, allowing it to move up and down as we open our mouth. The lower jaw is the only skull bone that can move.

Human Body

The human skull is also famous! Skull symbolism refers to the attachment of symbolic meaning to the human skull.

In many New England graveyards, the skull can still be seen on many tombstones. Sometimes it is used with a pair of angel wings, as in this picture, symbolizing flying away from mortality.

Here lyes Buried the Body of

The skull has appeared in many films and plays, perhaps most famously for the part it played in Hamlet, by William Shakespeare. The skull belongs to Yorick, a court jester, whose skull is dug up by a gravedigger. When *Hamlet* sees the skull, he makes a famous speech about the effects of death.

SCAN ME
Instructions on page 5

"Alas, poor Yorick! I knew him, Horatio; a fellow of infinite jest, of most excellent fancy; he hath borne me on his back a thousand times; and now, how abhorred in my imagination it is! My gorge rises at it. Here hung those lips that I have kissed I know not how oft. Where be your gibes now? Your gambols? Your songs? Your flashes of merriment, that were wont to set the table on a roar?"

AHOY, ME HEARTIES!

Perhaps the most famous use of the human skull was when it appeared colored white, with two crossed bones underneath it on a black background. This image, known as the Jolly Roger, was used frequently as a flag by ships in the 18th century who wanted to signal that they were a pirate ship. Pirates were crew of a ship that conducted criminal robbery or violence at sea against other ships.

The Jolly Roger was often a way for pirates to signal their intentions and to scare other ships. One record of the Jolly Roger skull flag being used by a pirate was on the 2nd May, 1822 in the Florida Straits, USA. The Massachusetts brigantine, called the Belvidere, reported that it had fended off an attack by a schooner boat whilst sailing in the Florida Straits.

EWW, GROSS!

It is a lucky thing that most modern doctors no longer practice **trepanning** as a cure for cranial diseases, as otherwise a lot of people would be walking round with holey heads. Trepanning is the act of drilling or scraping a hole into the human head through the skull. Evidence has been found that this procedure has been carried out since the Stone Age and has continued as a form of treatment ever since, making trepanning the oldest surgical procedure supported by archeological evidence. Believe it or not, trepanning is still carried out today for certain brain injuries but rather than using old knives, like they did in the Stone Age, they now have diamond-coated drills to make the process quicker and provide a cleaner cut to the bone of the skull.

USEFUL PIRATE SPEAK

seadog - old pirate or sailor

Aaaarrrrgggghhhh! - an expression of disgust

Ahoy! - Hello!

aye – yes

cat O'Nine Tails - a whip with nine strands

Dead men tell no tales - phrase indicating to leave no survivors

landlubber - big, slow clumsy person who doesn't know how to sail

pieces of eight - silver coins found in pirate stashes

shiver me timbers! - an expression of surprise

THE MOUTH

Your marvellous mouth is a wonderfully designed machine. Not only is it one of the key parts of the digestive system but it also helps us to communicate. The mouth is lined with mucous membranes which protect the inside and keeps your mouth moist.

Your mouth is made up of the following basic parts:

upper jaw – that is part of the skull

lower jaw – connected with the upper jaw, with ability to move up–down and from side to side

teeth and gums

cheek muscles

tongue

salivary glands – these pour saliva into the mouth

WHY DOES YOUR MOUTH WATER?

Your mouth waters due to a slimy liquid called saliva. Three pairs of salivary glands in the walls and floor of the mouth secrete saliva to moisten the mouth when we eat to make it easier to chew and swallow. Saliva contains a digestive enzyme that helps us to break down carbohydrates (which are found in pasta and bread, for example) and makes food easier to digest.

DID YOU KNOW?

The average person in the West eats 50 tons of food and drinks 50,000 liters (11,000 gallons) of liquid during his life. It also takes food seven seconds to go from the mouth to the stomach via the esophagus.

DID YOU KNOW?

WHAT A LOT OF SALIVA!

Humans produce about 37,854 liters of saliva in an average life time.

WHY DO WE HAVE LIPS?

Our lips also perform many tasks, from helping to eat food, positioning food in the mouth, chewing and speaking. The lips are made up of muscle which allow mobility. They are covered with skin on the outside and with slippery mucous membranes on the inside. The reddish tint of our lips comes from blood vessels lying just under the surface, which is why the lips can bleed so easily if you hurt them.

DID YOU KNOW?

LICKING YOUR LIPS ACTUALLY MAKES THEM DRIER.

When your lips get dry, licking them may make them feel better in the short term, but it doesn't last very long. Exposure to water actually takes away moisture from your lips when the saliva evaporates, just like repeatedly washing your hands dries out your skin. Lip balm is much more effective!

SMILING IS AWESOME!

People who are smiling in school yearbooks are more likely to have successful careers and marriages than their non-smiling peers.

FUN FACT!

WHAT ARE TONSILS?

The tonsils are two balls of lymphatic tissue found at the back of the mouth. Their job is to help fight germs that come in through the mouth and nose, before they cause troublesome infections in the rest of the body.

People whose mouth has a narrow roof are more likely to snore. This is because they have less oxygen going through their nose.

17

TONGUE

The tongue is an amazing muscle that is linked to our sense of taste. Although our sense of taste doesn't keep us alive, just imagine how boring life would be if we couldn't taste things. Our tongues also help us to speak and digest our food.

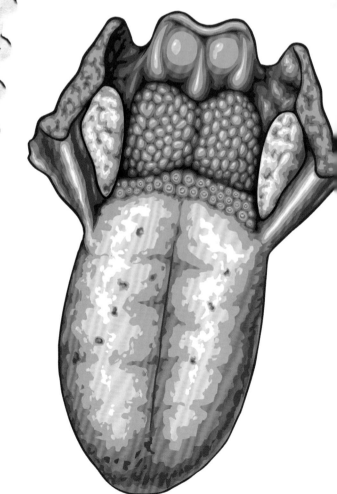

HOW WE TASTE

Saliva in our mouths helps dissolve the food we eat. The food then washes over the surface of the tongue, which is covered in taste buds. We have over 10,000 taste buds, which help us detect the five basic tastes in food.

sweet - foods containing sugar such as fruit

salty - foods such as oysters, tuna, chips and fries

sour - foods such as lemon and vinegar

bitter - foods such as kale, radicchio, rocket and coffee

savory - umami are savory tastes often found in meat, fish, vegetables and dairy products

18

TRY THIS AT HOME!

Try this experiment at home with a friend. Take it in turns to close your eyes and feed each other different types of food. Can you tell which taste each food has without looking at it?

DID YOU KNOW?

That smoking cigarettes is not only very bad for you, it also deadens the taste buds. There is also evidence to prove nicotine found in cigarettes suppresses nerve activity in areas of the brain associated with taste.

SPEAKING AND THE TONGUE

The tongue has other functions as well as helping us to taste, such as helping us to speak. Muscles in the back of our tongues help us to make certain sounds, like the letters 'r', 'k' and 'g'. Next time you are speaking, concentrate on the movements your tongue makes. Can you feel how it moves against the top of your mouth to create the sounds?

DIGESTION AND OUR TONGUE

Our tongues also help us to digest our food. Once the food is all ground up, mixed with saliva and thoroughly tasted of course, our tongues help us to push food into the esophagus, which is the pipe that leads from your throat to your stomach.

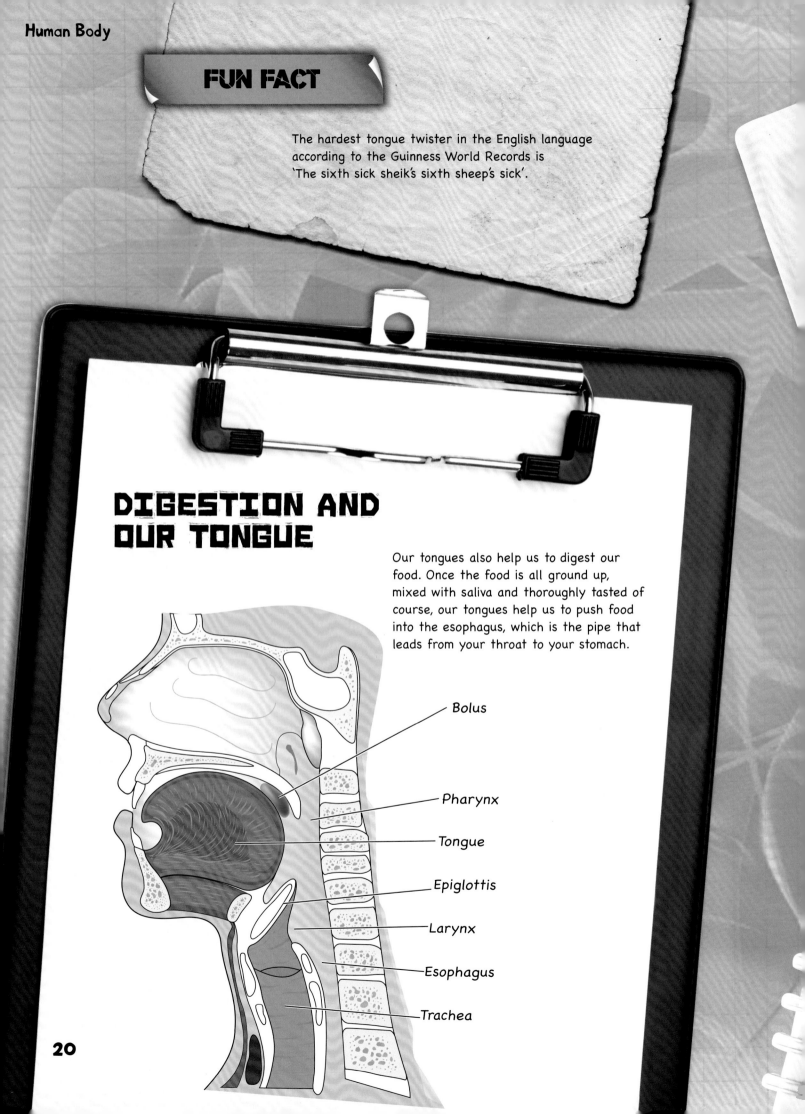

Bolus

Pharynx

Tongue

Epiglottis

Larynx

Esophagus

Trachea

EWW, GROSS!

The saying 'has the cat got your tongue' came from Assyria over 2500 years ago, where criminals had their tongues cut out and they were fed to the king's cat.

DID YOU KNOW?

Women have shorter tongues than men.

TONGUE MYTH

Some people believe that being able to roll your tongue into a tube is a genetic trait, however recent studies have shown that it isn't in fact genetic at all.

THE TEETH

Our teeth help us to bite and chew food, just imagine how difficult it would be to eat an apple without them! First teeth start to appear in babies at between 6 and 12 months, these teeth are called milk teeth and most children will have 20 teeth by the age of three years old. At the age of five or six, the first teeth start to fall out to make way for the larger adult teeth. By the age of 14, most people will have a set of 28 adult teeth. Between the ages of 17 to 21, the final four teeth called wisdom teeth appear, although not everyone gets these.

TYPES OF TEETH

There are four different types of teeth, each designed to do a different job.

- Incisors are used for cutting and chopping food and are the front four teeth at the top and bottom of the jaw.
- Canine teeth are used for tearing food. There are four of them, one each side of the incisors.
- Premolars are used for crushing and grinding food. There are eight of them and they are found next to the canine teeth at the top and bottom of the jaw.
- Molars are used for mashing food. There are eight of these and they are found next to the premolars at the top and bottom of the jaw.

WHAT IS INSIDE OUR TEETH?

Inside our teeth are lots of nerves and blood vessels. This is why we get toothache and can feel hot and cold if these nerves become exposed.

HOW COOL!

TOOTH FACT

The outside of the tooth is made of enamel, which is the toughest substance in our body. Enamel doesn't contain any living cells so cannot be repaired if damaged, which is why it is important to look after your teeth.

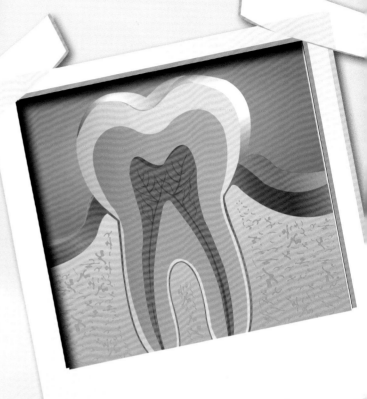

HOW DO OUR TEETH STAY IN?

Our teeth are held in by long roots. These roots are surrounded by a kind of cement that holds them firmly in place within our jaws.

TOOTH CARE

Teeth can decay if they are not looked after properly. Bacteria from food can get stuck between teeth and turn into something called plaque that eats away at the tooth enamel. Brushing your teeth twice a day and regular visits to the dentist help to keep your teeth healthy.

DID YOU KNOW?

No two people have the same set of teeth. Like your fingerprints, your teeth are unique. Forensic dentists are sometimes used to examine teeth for clues to somebody's identity if no other forms of identification are possible.

EYES

Sight is the human body's main sense. Although we can function without sight, we rely on our eyes to learn about our surroundings. From the moment we wake up until we go to sleep at night, our eyes are in constant use. We use our eyes for almost every activity we do from writing, reading, watching TV, to crossing the road, the list is endless! Our eyes help us to determine shapes, colors, movement and much more. Around two-thirds of the information our brains receive comes from our eyes. This information travels along the optic nerve and goes to the brain. Then the information is processed by our brain, which helps us to make decisions. For example, if you see a ball flying towards you, you will move out of the way quickly!

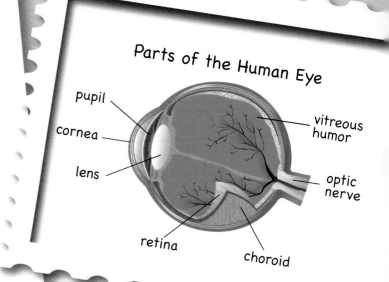

Parts of the Human Eye

pupil
cornea
lens
retina
vitreous humor
optic nerve
choroid

DID YOU KNOW?

Our eyes are made up of watery jelly and are very fragile, so they need to be well protected. Luckily, our bodies have given us some protection. Our skulls are made of bone, which protects the brain and the back of the eye. Most of our eye is encased in the eye socket and has the extra protection of layers of fat.

Our eyebrows prevent sweat from dripping into our eyes.

Our eyelids and eyelashes help stop dust and dirt going into our eyes.

AWESOME

The iris – the colored part of your eye – is as unique as a fingerprint.. Some airports now have hi-tech eye scanners as a way of identifying people quickly.

EYE MYTH!

SITTING TOO CLOSE TO THE TV IS BAD FOR YOUR EYES.

A famous phrase from parents all over the world, but it isn't true. There is no evidence that sitting close to a television will damage your eyes. Watching television won't give you square eyes either!

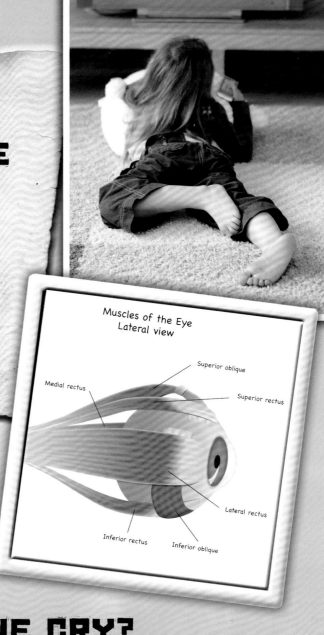

Muscles of the Eye
Lateral view

Medial rectus

Superior oblique

Superior rectus

Lateral rectus

Inferior rectus

Inferior oblique

HOW DO YOUR EYES STAY IN?

Six muscles firmly attach each eye to your skull. These are called the medial and lateral rectus, the superior and inferior oblique and the superior and inferior rectus muscles.

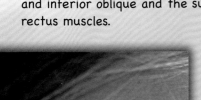

WHY DO WE CRY?

Tear ducts are small glands inside your upper eyelid. They produce a salty liquid that forms tears. Tears lubricate and protect our eyes from dust and other particles and help keep them clean.

Did you know that there are three types of tears generated by the human eye?

Basal tears protect the eye and keep it moist.

Reflex tears flush out the eye when it becomes irritated.

Emotional tears flow in response to sadness, distress, or physical pain.

Studies have shown crying can be good for you! It relieves tension by balancing the body's stress levels.

WHAT DOES THE PUPIL DO?

The pupil is the black part in the middle of your eye. It is an opening that controls how much light enters the eye. The pupil gets smaller in bright light to protect the nerve cells and larger in darkness to let more light in so we can see.

Did you know that the pupil gets bigger if you see something you like?

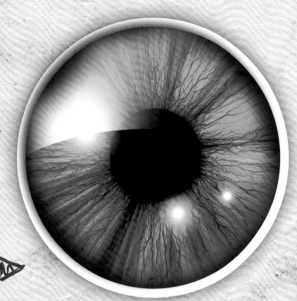

HOW YOUR EYES WORK

Your eye works in a similar way to the lens in a camera. Like a camera, light passes through the pupil (the lens) of your eye and is recorded on the back of your eye (the retina). The image is upside down and the cells in the eye pass messages down the optic nerve to the brain. The brain then translates the image, flips it back the right way round and processes the information about the image.

THE SEEING CELLS

Our eyes have millions of cells that help to process the images we see. These cells are called rods and cones. Rods see images in black and white and work well in dim light. Cones can see detail and colors but only work well in bright light. The function of rods and cones is to turn an image into an electrical message for our brain.

Did you know that each eye contains about 120 million rods and 6 million cones?

EYE MYTH

EATING CARROTS WILL IMPROVE YOUR VISION

Fact: The benefits of eating carrots may have been slightly exaggerated in World War II. The British, in an effort to keep their newly developed radar secret, spread the word that the reason British pilots were able to perform so well at night was they ate lots of carrots! What really helps your eyesight is vitamin A and while carrots contain vitamin A, they only provide you with a small amount.

Other foods high in vitamin A are milk, cheese, egg yolk, and liver.

VISION PROBLEMS

Some people have problems with their eyes and their eyesight is not perfect. Eyesight problems are often caused by a refractive error occurring when the shape of the eye prevents it from focusing light correctly, resulting in a blurred image. Some of the most common eyesight problems include:

Nearsighted – this is where you have difficulty seeing things at a distance

Farsighted – this is where you have difficulty seeing things close up

Color blind – this is where you cannot see certain colors, especially green and red. This is often more common in men than women.

Most common eye problems, such as those mentioned above, can be fixed by wearing glasses, contact lenses or sometimes having eye surgery.

DID YOU KNOW?

Eye specialists who test your eyes for vision problems are called optometrists. It is recommended that you get your eyes checked at least every two years.

MORE SERIOUS PROBLEMS

Cataracts are the world's leading cause of blindness and around 18 million people have gone blind as a result of cataracts. They are caused by a clouding of the lens inside the eye which leads to a decrease in vision. Although cataracts are quite a common problem found all over the world, getting treatment is much more difficult in developing countries. Cataracts affect children as well as adults and sadly many people have gone blind because they do not know that they can be cured.

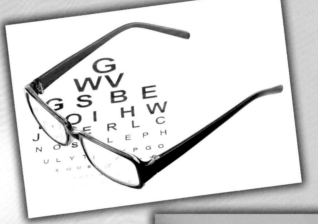

Eye diseases

Clear lens

Normal

Cataract

Cloudy lens

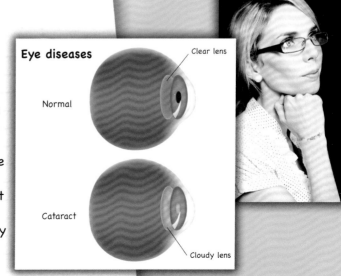

27

EARS

Our ears are part of a clever system that enables us to hear sounds. They act a little like satellite dishes, picking up different sound waves and transmitting them into our ear canals. Our ears convert these sound waves when they travel through the tiny hairs inside the cochlea and changes them into nerve impulses, like electrical messages which are sent to the brain. The brain then decodes and makes sense of the sounds we hear.

Our ears are made up of three parts which work together to help us hear sounds:

- The outer ear: this is the part we can see. It collects and funnels sound inwards.

- The middle ear: contains the eardrum, and three tiny bones called the hammer, anvil and stirrup causing vibrations.

- The inner ear translates the sound vibrations to nerve impulses for the brain.

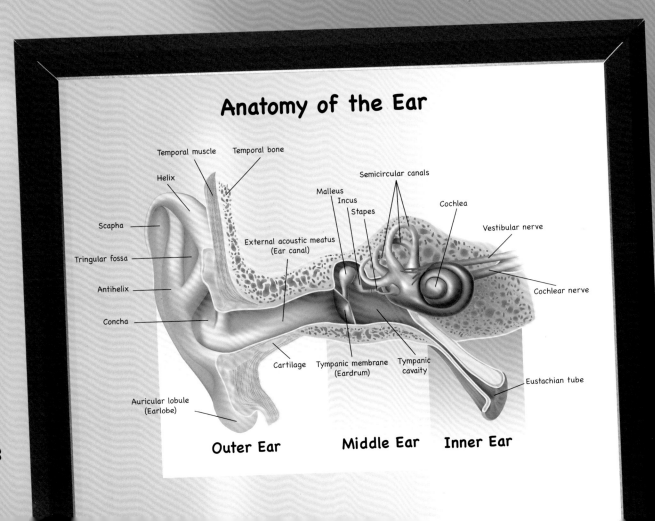

Anatomy of the Ear

Temporal muscle
Temporal bone
Helix
Semicircular canals
Malleus
Incus
Cochlea
Stapes
Scapha
Vestibular nerve
External acoustic meatus
(Ear canal)
Tringular fossa
Antihelix
Cochlear nerve
Concha
Cartilage
Tympanic membrane
(Eardrum)
Tympanic
cavaity
Eustachian tube
Auricular lobule
(Earlobe)

Outer Ear   **Middle Ear**   **Inner Ear**

SOUND

Sound is a type of energy made by vibrations and these vibrations are called sound waves. When an object vibrates it causes movement in the air particles and if your ear is within range of these vibrations, you hear the sound. Humans can hear a wide range of sounds from high notes to low notes. Children can hear much higher ranges of notes than adults and the range of notes you hear shrinks with age.

BALANCE

Our ears also help us to keep our balance. Canals inside our ears contain fluid and as you move the fluid flows around. Tiny hairs act as sensors to tell the brain which way up you are.

WHY DO WE HAVE

EWW, GROSS!

EARWAX?

Earwax is a sticky yellow wax made in the outer ear. Although a little gross, it is extremely useful. It contains chemicals that help us fight infections, it keeps our ears moist so they don't get itchy and also collects dirt to stop it travelling further inside our ear.

Ear piercing isn't just a recent trend. Humans have been piercing their ears since prehistoric times. Ötzi, a 5,300-year-old iceman

AWESOME!

SCAN ME
Instructions on page 5

who was found mummified in an Alpine glacier in 1991, had both ears pierced.

The ear continues to hear sounds, even while you sleep.

EAR MYTH

A. Some people believe that large ears give you an increased ability to pick up information, making you smarter. However, this isn't true. Hearing is made possible from the structures within your ear!

If you sit in front of the speakers at a rock concert you could be exposing yourself to over 120 decibels of sound. This will begin to damage hearing in only 7 1/2 minutes.

Q. Do bigger ears mean you are more intelligent?

DID YOU KNOW?

WATCH OUT!

NECK

Our amazing neck supports the head and also connects our head to our torso. It is defined as the region that starts at the bottom of the lower jaw and finishes at the clavicle, or collar bone. The neck is one of the most complex areas of the body and contains many vital structures, including the spinal cord and thyroid gland, and these are closely packed together within layers of connective tissue. The structure of the neck is composed of muscles, ligaments and the 7 cervical vertebrae.

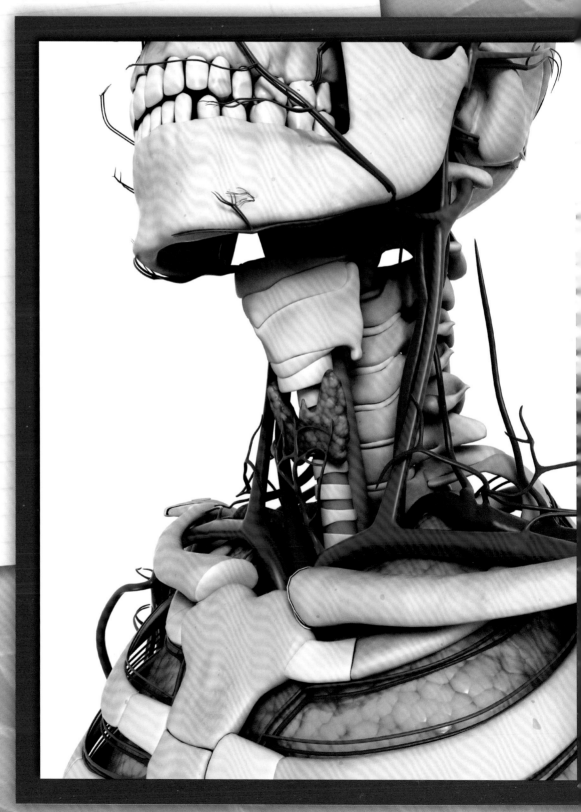

MAJOR PARTS CONTAINED WITHIN THE NECK

The muscles that run up the front of the neck are divided into the suprahyoid and infrahyoid muscle groups. These muscles are attached to the hyoid bone and raise and lower this bone and the larynx during swallowing.

The thyroid gland produces thyroid hormones that increase the metabolic rate of body cells. The thyroid gland consists of two lobes on both sides of the trachea and esophagus.

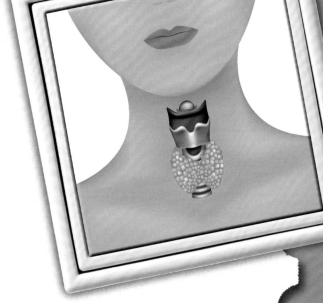

The internal jugular veins and carotid arteries are located in the neck.

Parathyroid glands are small glands which are located in the neck behind the thyroid. There are usually four of them and they control the amount of calcium in our bodies.

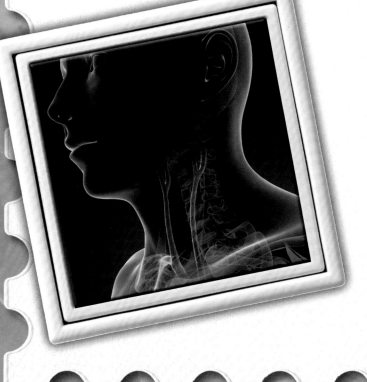

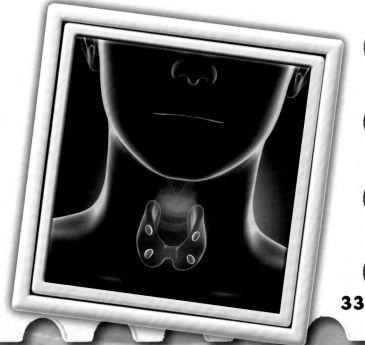

PHARYNX

The pharynx, located at the back of the throat, is a passage way both for food to the digestive system and air to the lungs. The entrance to the pharynx is guarded by the tonsils.

FUN FACT

The Adam's apple is named after the story of the Garden of Eden where Adam ate a piece of the forbidden fruit (which people say was an apple) that got stuck in his throat.

LARYNX

The larynx is more commonly called the voice box It houses the vocal cords and is like our sound production studio, manipulating volume and pitch. It also protects the trachea against food leakage and is involved in breathing. When the larynx grows larger during puberty, it sticks out at the front of the throat. Everyone's larynx grows during puberty, but a girl's larynx doesn't grow as big as a boy's does. That's why boys have Adam's apples and girls don't.

TRACHEA

The trachea, or windpipe, is the tube that connects the nose and mouth to the lungs.

The Lymphatic System

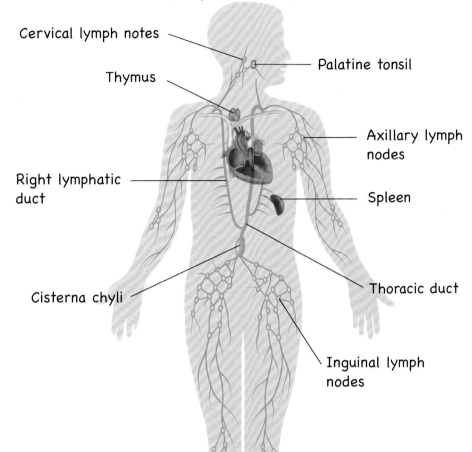

Cervical lymph notes

Palatine tonsil

Thymus

Axillary lymph nodes

Right lymphatic duct

Spleen

Cisterna chyli

Thoracic duct

Inguinal lymph nodes

LYMPHATIC DUCTS

The left and right lymphatic ducts are the major lymphatic vessels. They collect lymph from the left or right side of the neck, chest, and arm, and empty it into a large vein on the left or right side of the neck.

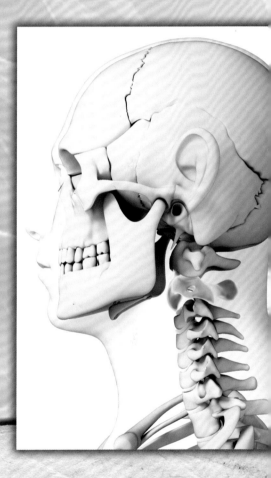

FUN FACTS

Humans and giraffes have the same number of neck (cervical) vertebrae.

The top cervical vertebrae allows you to move your head up and down and the second cervical vertebrae allows you to move your head from side to side.

Neck bones feature a pivot joint and this allows our heads to turn.

One of the main functions of the neck is to protect the nerves that are between our brain and the rest of the human body.

According to the Guinness World Records, the longest human neck is 16 inches (40 cm). It was created by adding successive copper coils to the neck over a number of years. The women of the Padaung or Kareni tribe of Myanmar add them as a sign of beauty.

35

THROAT

Our throat is a muscular tube, like a passageway, that runs down the neck taking the food we eat and the air we breathe down into our bodies. The throat is found behind the nose and mouth. At the bottom of the throat it splits into two parts, the first, the esophagus which takes food to the stomach and the second, the larynx which takes air to the lungs. The throat also contains our voice box which helps us to form speech.

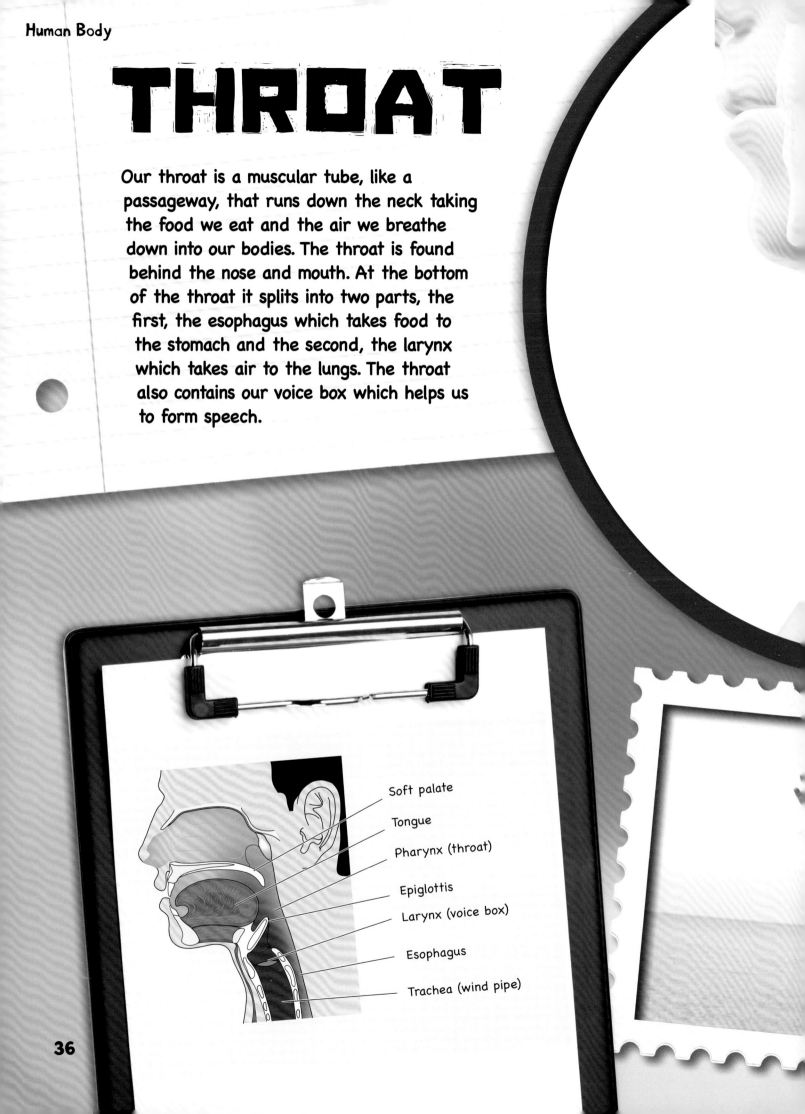

Soft palate

Tongue

Pharynx (throat)

Epiglottis

Larynx (voice box)

Esophagus

Trachea (wind pipe)

DID YOU KNOW?

WHAT HAPPENS WHEN YOU SWALLOW?

Swallowing is a reflex action which happens automatically without us having to think about it. When we swallow, a small ball of chewed up food or liquids is pushed by our tongue into the back of the mouth where it enters the throat. A special flap called the epiglottis comes down over the opening of your windpipe to make sure the food travels safely into the esophagus and not the windpipe.

WHAT HAPPENS TO THE AIR IN OUR THROAT?

After air is taken in through the nose or mouth, it will travel down the throat, down the windpipe which is held open by cartilage rings, and into the lungs.

WHAT HAPPENS WHEN FOOD GOES DOWN THE WRONG PIPE?

Sometimes on rare occasions when we are laughing or messing about when we eat, the epiglottis doesn't shut in time and our food goes down our windpipe. When this happens we naturally cough to expel the food. It can be very scary but usually we are fine after a few seconds and the food is coughed back out of the windpipe.

However food or an object can get stuck in the windpipe and this is called choking. It is very serious as the person will be unable to breathe as air cannot flow to the lungs.

WHAT IS THE HEIMLICH MANEUVER?

The Heimlich maneuver (abdominal thrusts) is a three-step emergency technique that can save a life in seconds if you are choking. It is a simple action that will often dislodge food or another object from a person's airway when they are choking. It involves placing an increase in pressure in the abdomen and chest, enabling the object to be expelled. It is well worth learning this technique in a first aid course.

HOW DOES OUR VOICE BOX WORK?

The voice box is known as the larynx and it is found at the top of the windpipe. When you speak or make a noise, the vocal cords vibrate as you exhale and a sound is created. The noise made by the larynx combined with the shape of your mouth gives each person a unique sounding voice. The way we move our mouth, tongue and lips, changes the way the noise from larynx will sound. Controlling vocal cords and changing the pitch of your voice is something we all learn as an infant when we start to talk. Singers control their vocal cords in order to help them sing.

WHY DO WE GET A SORE THROAT?

A sore throat is a common problem, and is usually the result of a bacterial or viral infection. Most of the time a sore throat usually resolves itself without complications, but it sometimes does require treatment with an antibiotic. However there are some less common causes of sore throat that are serious or even life-threatening.

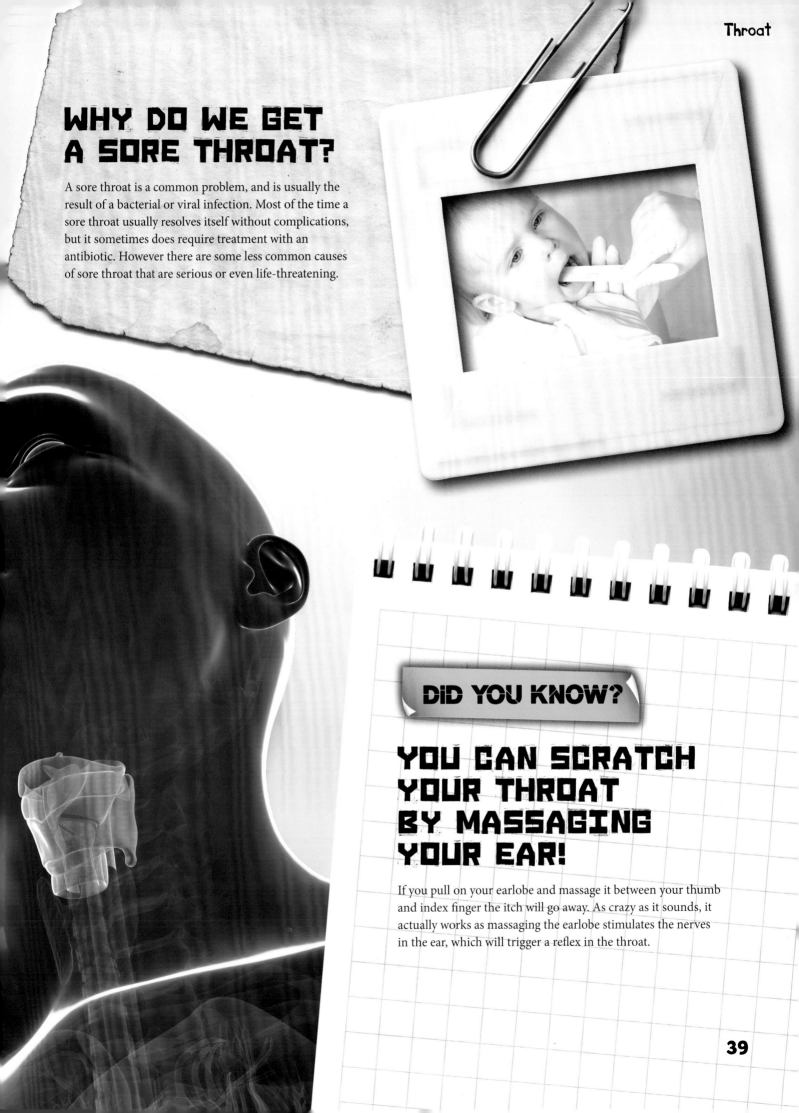

DID YOU KNOW?

YOU CAN SCRATCH YOUR THROAT BY MASSAGING YOUR EAR!

If you pull on your earlobe and massage it between your thumb and index finger the itch will go away. As crazy as it sounds, it actually works as massaging the earlobe stimulates the nerves in the ear, which will trigger a reflex in the throat.

SKIN

Your skin is perhaps the most remarkable part of your body. It really is like magic. It is also very important as it covers and protects everything inside your body. Imagine if you had no skin at all – your muscles, bones and organs would all be on show and falling out. The skin does more than just hold everything in place, it protects our bodies, keeps our body at the right temperature and also allows us to have the sense of touch.

DID YOU KNOW?

Did you know that the skin is the biggest organ in your body?

LAYERS

The skin has three layers with the top layer called the epidermis, the next layer the dermis and the bottom layer subcutaneous. Each layer has a part to play in the functioning of the skin.

Human Skin Anatomy

Sweat pore

Hair

Sebaceous gland

Epidermis

Hair bulb

Hair muscle

Arteriole

Dermis

Venule

Apocrine sweat gland

Sensory nerve

Motor nerve

Hypodermis– Subcutaneous fat

EPIDERMIS

The epidermis, the top layer, is the layer of skin you can see. It is constantly replenishing itself by creating new skin cells which travel to the top part of the epidermis layer when they are ready. As they move to the top of the epidermis the older cells near the top start to die and move even closer to the surface of the skin. When they reach the surface these skin cells are already dead and become strong and tough. They are perfect as a protective coating.

THAT MAKES MY SKIN CRAWL

The skin you see all over your body is actually dead skin cells at the surface. These dead cells flake off and every minute you lose around 35,000 dead skin cells. That means you shed around 9 lb (4 kg) over the course of a year.

COOL FACT!

Around 95% of the skin cells in the epidermis are tasked with creating new skin cells to replace the old ones. The other 5% of cells produce melanin which gives skin its color. The more melanin in your skin the darker skin color you have. These cells produce melanin to protect your skin from being burned by the sun's ultraviolet (UV) rays.

DERMIS

Underneath the epidermis lies the dermis which contains all the nerve endings, blood vessels, oil glands and sweat glands as well as collagen and elastin.

Blood Vessels – There are many tiny blood vessels in the dermis which keep your skin cells healthy by bringing oxygen and nutrients and taking away waste. As you get older your dermis starts to get thinner and so you may be able to see these blood vessels when you are older.

Sweat & Oil Glands – The oil glands in the dermis are also called the sebaceous glands. They produce sebum which is your skin's natural oil. This oil rises to the surface and makes the skin waterproof. The sweat glands produce sweat that passes to the surface through pores, which are tiny holes in the skin. Sweat and sebum combined create a sticky yet protective film over the skin.

Nerve Endings – The nerve endings in your dermis connect directly to your central nervous system and brain. This way the skin can protect you from touching harmful things. If you touch something that is hot and will damage the skin the nerve endings immediately relay that message to the brain which flexes the required muscles to make you pull your hand away without even thinking about it. These nerve endings in the dermis are not just there to protect, they also allow us to feel what you are touching. They will send messages to the brain about what you are touching, so you know the texture and temperature of what you are touching. There's a big difference between touching an ice cube and brushing your hand on hot sand on a beach.

SUBCUTANEOUS

The final layer of skin at the bottom is the subcutaneous. This multi-purpose layer helps bind your skin to the tissue beneath it, such as your muscles, but also helps your body stay warm and absorb any shocks.

It is mostly made up of fat and is also where every follicle starts. A follicle is a tiny tube in the skin where hair grows from. Hair follicles are all over your body and each has a sebaceous gland attached to it in the dermis layer that releases sebum onto the hair. This gives the hair a coating of oil and make it slightly waterproof.

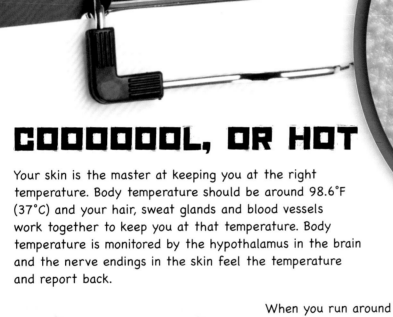

COOOOOOL, OR HOT

Your skin is the master at keeping you at the right temperature. Body temperature should be around 98.6°F (37°C) and your hair, sweat glands and blood vessels work together to keep you at that temperature. Body temperature is monitored by the hypothalamus in the brain and the nerve endings in the skin feel the temperature and report back.

When you run around on a hot day the report back to the brain suggests that you are overheating so the hypothalamus sends a signal out to cool down and release some of your body's heat. Straight away your blood vessels start bringing warm blood closer to the surface. This is why you get a red face if exercising hard. Sweat glands also start making lots of sweat to release your body heat into the air. It does this by creating sweat that evaporates into the air, which through energy exchange cools you down.

If your skin reports back to the hypothalamus that you are cold then the message goes out to reserve your body heat. Your skin does this by trying to keep as much warm blood away from the surface as possible. This can result in goosebumps which are tiny bumps on your skin. The technical term for goosebumps is the pilomotor reflex. This is where tiny muscles called the erector pili muscles pull on the hairs which makes them stand up straight.

NAILS

Don't bite your nails, treasure them, they are very special. We have nails on all of our fingers and toes. The skin cells in your fingers and toes produce the nails, which are there to protect the finger tips from damage. They also make your finger tips more sensitive as any pressure applied meets a counter-force pressure from the nail on the top so the pressure on the pad of the finger is enhanced. Your nails are also used as a tool. You can use them to scratch and you can also use them as a grip on fiddly little items - think about trying to pull out a splinter from your finger.

Nails are made from the skin cells in the fingers and toes, which produce a hardened protein called keratin. This is the same material that makes up your hair and is also found in other areas of the skin. The nails grow from an area called the matrix where the new cells are produced and push out the older cells. The older cells become compacted and then form the flattened, hardened finger or toe nail.

The nail is actually formed of several parts:

nail plate - The nail itself that you can see

nail bed - The skin underneath the nail plate

cuticle - The tissue that overlaps the plate and rims the base of the nail

nail folds - The skin folds that frame and support the nail on three sides

matrix - The part of the nail unit under the cuticle that you cannot see

DID YOU KNOW?

Your fingernails grow faster than your toenails.

Younger people's nails grow faster.

Males' nails grow faster than females'.

Your nails grow faster in the summer.

If you are right-handed, the fingernails on your right hand will grow faster than your left and vice versa.

NICE NAILS

People often decorate their nails with polish to make them look pretty. This has been dated back to at least 3000 BC. A cosmetic procedure called a manicure (hands) and a pedicure (feet) is where a nail technician uses tools to groom, trim and paint the nail.

HOW COOL!

ITCHY AND SCRATCHY

The Guinness world record for the longest nail is held by Shridhar Chillal from India who set the record in 1998 with a thumb nail of 4.8 feet (1.5 m) long. The closest female record holder is Lee Redmond from the USA who had a thumb nail of 2 feet 11 inches (89 cm) in 2008.

YUK!

There are many specific diseases of the nails where infection can cause discoloration, brittleness, thickening, abnormal growths and more. Deformity or disease of the nails is called onychosis.

A HAIRY STORY

Hair comes in all shapes and sizes and is all over your body. It is important not only for your body as it relays sensory information but is also used in appearance, making you look good. Human hair is even cut, collected and sold on for others to use in extensions across the world. Believe it or not, all of your hair follicles are formed before you are born, when you are a fetus of around 22 weeks. You have around 5 million hair follicles on your body and around 100,000 on the scalp.

STRUCTURE

Hair is made up of a **follicle** that you cannot see and the **shaft** which is the bit you can see.

Follicle - The follicle is a tube that goes from the skin surface all the way down to the **subcutaneous** layer in the skin. At the bottom of the tube there is the **bulb**, the living part of the hair. The bulb is fed by blood vessels right at the bottom section. The bulb is the engine room of the hair and the cells there produce new cells faster than any other cells in the body. The follicle is surrounded by two protective sheaths, an inner and an outer sheath. The inner sheath only comes up to where the **oil gland (sebaceous gland)** is. This gland produces **sebum**, which is a conditioner for the hair to keep it healthy and slightly waterproof. There is also a small muscle attached to the follicle called the **pili muscle**. When this contracts it makes the hair stand up – this is what happens when you get **goosebumps**.

Shaft – Just like your nails, the hair shaft is made up of a hard protein called **keratin**. The hair is not living tissue as the keratin protein has died and hardened. There are three layers of keratin that make up the hair. The inner layer is called the **medulla**. The next layer is the **cortex** and this makes up most of the hair shaft and is where pigment cells are located to give the hair its color. The **cuticle** is the last layer and this is actually formed by tightly packed overlapping scales.

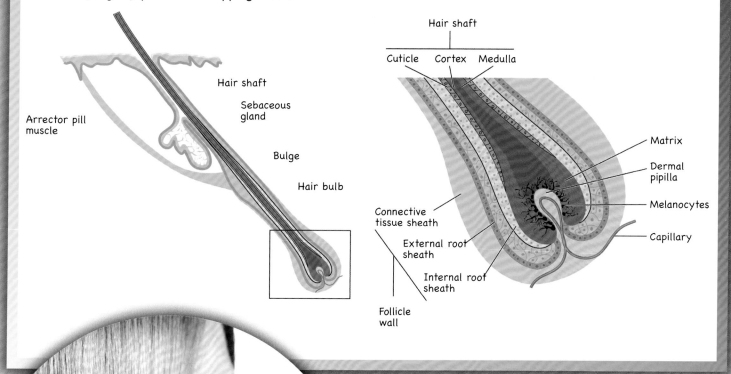

Hair shaft

Arrector pill muscle

Hair shaft

Sebaceous gland

Bulge

Hair bulb

Cuticle   Cortex   Medulla

Matrix

Dermal pipilla

Melanocytes

Capillary

Connective tissue sheath

External root sheath

Internal root sheath

Follicle wall

SMOOTH CONDITIONER

Hair conditioner is used by many people to make their hair feel smooth and shiny. Most hair conditioners try to smooth the scales of the cuticle layer on the hair.

I HAIR-ED IT ALL BEFORE

What makes music on your hair?

Head bands

HAIR GROWTH

Hair is always being replenished by your body in a cycle. This means that right now there will be hairs that you will be shedding but also hairs that have just started growing. There are three stages of hair growth: **catagen**, **telogen**, and **anagen**.

Catagen – 3% of hairs are in this stage at any one time. This stage lasts for about three weeks.

Telogen – The next stage is Telogen phase. Around 10-15% of hairs are in this stage which lasts for around 99 days. The hair follicle rests during this stage.

Anagen - During the Anagen phase, the cells in the root of the hair are busy producing more cells. These new hair cells push the older cells up and out of the skin. The hair grows very fast during this stage – around 1 cm every month. Scalp hair is the most active and can stay in this active phase for 2-7 years. The hair on the arms, legs and eyebrows has a shorter active phase (35 days) which is why they are shorter.

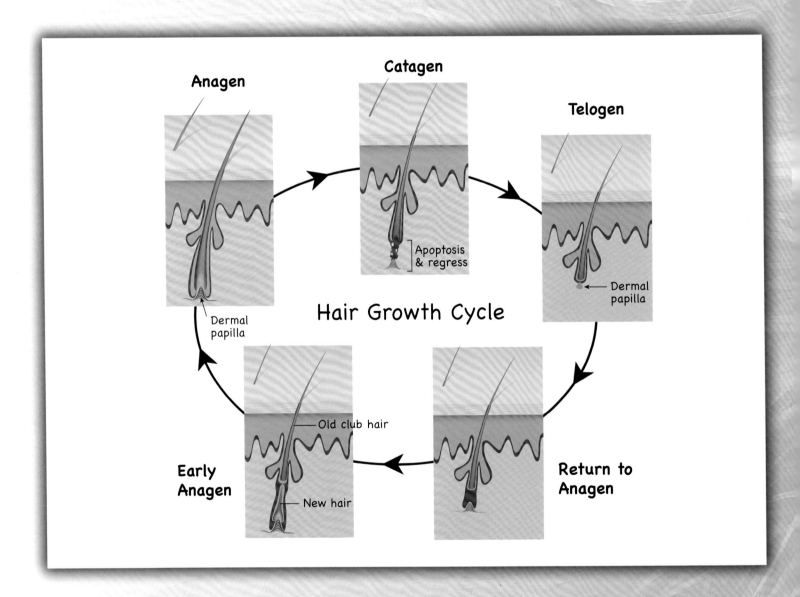

MY HAIR IS FASTER THAN YOURS

People can have hair with different active growth phases than others. This is why some people can grow their hair long relatively quickly in comparison to others – who will have a shorter active phase in their hair.

SCALP FACT

Hair on the scalp grows about 0.35 mm each day which is about 15 cm or 6 inches per year!

UNIQUELY HUMAN

Hair growth on humans is not seasonal or cyclic, growth and loss is completely at random.

CURLY WURLY

The cross-sectional shape of the hair determines how curly a person's hair is. If the hair cross section is quite flat it is more likely to be curly, if it is more circular then the hair will be straight. The shape of the hair also affects how shiny the hair is, straighter hair means more sebum can travel down the hair so therefore it is shinier.

HAIR STYLES

SCAN ME
Instructions on page 5

We style our hair in an enormous amount of different ways.
Look at some of the most popular hair styles over the past few decades:

60s

70s

Today

80s

90s

THORAX

The thorax is the technical name for the chest. This includes the rib-cage and everything it encases. From the neck and shoulders down to the abdomen there are some of the most incredible natural machines. These ingenious biological machines are the thorax organs such as the beating heart and the breathing lungs.

DID YOU KNOW?

ANIMALS

The thorax of most crustaceans (including lobsters and shrimps) and spiders and other arachnids is fused with the head into a cephalothorax. For vertebrates (animals which have a spine), the thorax is made up of the ribs, sternum (breastbone), and certain vertebrae of the backbone. It contains the heart, lungs and portions of the trachea and esophagus. In mammals, the thorax is separated from the abdomen by a thin muscular partition called the diaphragm. In humans, the thorax is called the chest.

BBQ RIBS

OK, not a good idea to try and BBQ your own ribs but did you know that the 12 ribs that form the cage are all uniquely shaped? Most have a head that fits into the vertebrae, a neck that is a flat section and a shaft that attaches to several intercostal muscles.

HOW MANY?

If you count your ribs there are normally 24 with 12 on the right and 12 on the left side. However, some people are born with one less or one more and it has no great effect on their wellbeing.

THORACIC FACTS

The thoracic cage is conical in shape which means it is narrow at the top and broad at the bottom. This is what helps give your upper body shape.

The costal cartilage are fibrous tissues that allow the thoracic cage to expand. When air comes into the lungs, the lungs inflate and the thoracic cage expands to accommodate them.

ABDOMEN

The abdomen is the trunk of the body. It is also known as the 'belly'! It is everything from the **diaphragm** in the chest to the **pelvis**. It contains all of the organs that digest your food suchas the **stomach, small** and **large intestines, pancreas, gallbladder** and **liver**.
It also contains the **kidneys** and the **spleen**.

All of the organs in the abdomen are held together by tissue. This tissue is flexible enough to allow the organs to glide across each other and expand. There are also many important blood vessels, like the aorta, that go through the abdomen.

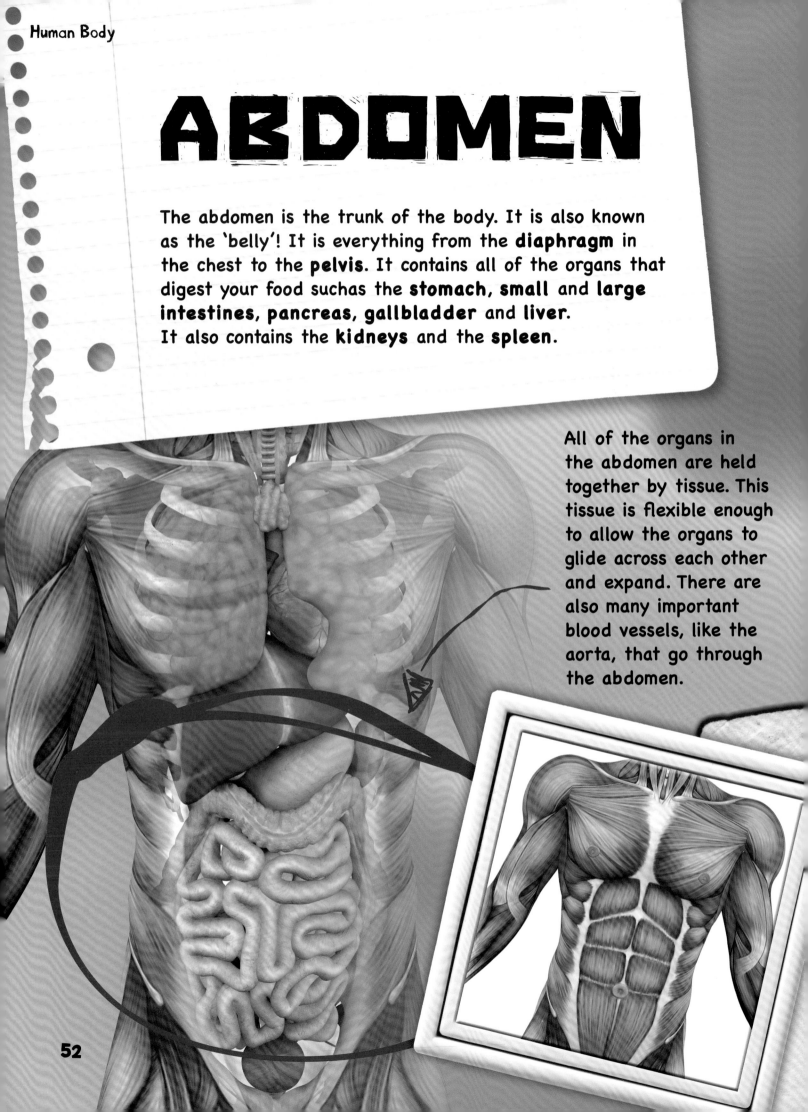

6 PACK PROTECTION

As there are so many important organs and blood vessels in the abdomen, they need to be protected well. The abdominal muscles play a major part in this but they also have many different functions. In conjunction with the back muscles they also provide support for the posture.

In fact the abdominal muscles and the muscles on the corresponding back section are responsible for supporting our delicate spine and for all our forward, backward and sideways leaning motion. They are so strong and flexible we can do the 'hula' and rotate our lower body whilst keeping our upper body fixed.

The abdominal muscles are also used for a variety of bodily functions. You use some of these muscles when you cough, urinate, defecate and vomit. They help us breathe and are critical in the singing process. Many professional singers are taught to 'sing from the belly' as they use these muscles to control breathing and therefore the air being released from their mouth.

DID YOU KNOW?

The famous 6-pack should be an 8-pack as there are four vertical sections on each side. However the bottom two sections are just above the pubic bone, so only six of the sections are visible. The muscle that forms the 6-pack is the **rectus abdominus**. To get the 6-pack look, you have to be very fit, eat well and exercise like this guy!

BODY SYSTEMS

The human body is a very complex biological machine. There are many continuous processes and systems going on that work together to make human life work.

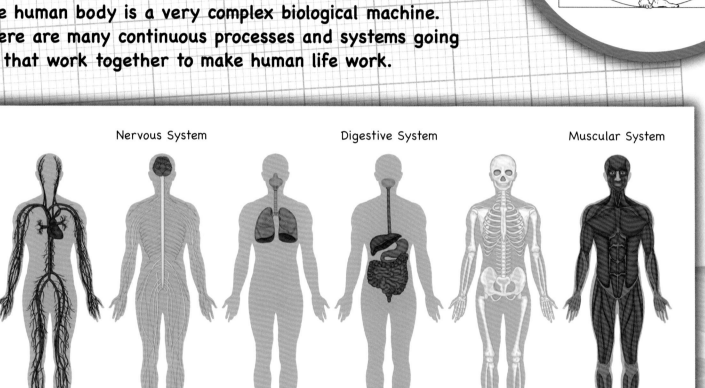

Nervous System

Digestive System

Muscular System

Circulatory System

Respiratory System

Skeletal System

CARDIOVASCULAR SYSTEM

The cardiovascular or circulatory system is the process that moves blood around our body. Blood acts like a delivery truck taking nutrients, hormones and most importantly oxygen around the whole body. After dropping off the 'goods' it loads up on waste products, like carbon dioxide (formed from used up oxygen) and takes these to be disposed of as well as to be reloaded with oxygen for another round-trip.

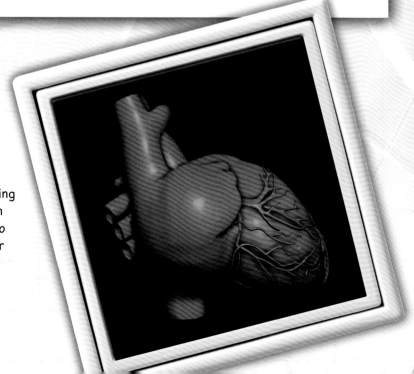

54

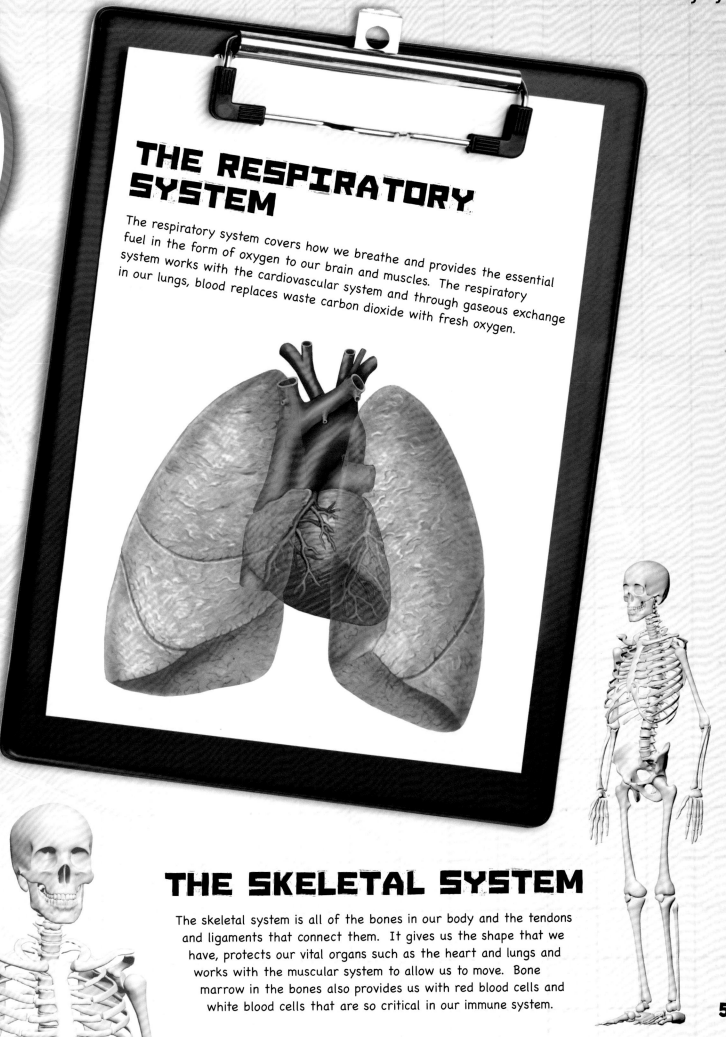

THE RESPIRATORY SYSTEM

The respiratory system covers how we breathe and provides the essential fuel in the form of oxygen to our brain and muscles. The respiratory system works with the cardiovascular system and through gaseous exchange in our lungs, blood replaces waste carbon dioxide with fresh oxygen.

THE SKELETAL SYSTEM

The skeletal system is all of the bones in our body and the tendons and ligaments that connect them. It gives us the shape that we have, protects our vital organs such as the heart and lungs and works with the muscular system to allow us to move. Bone marrow in the bones also provides us with red blood cells and white blood cells that are so critical in our immune system.

THE DIGESTIVE SYSTEM

The digestive system deals with how we process the food that we eat. It starts as soon as we put something in our mouths and goes down our throats. From there the food is broken down by acid and enzymes in the stomach releasing the fuel and nutrients it provides our body, which is absorbed through the intestinal walls. It is broken down further through the intestines and finally the solid waste reaches the end of a 9-meter long journey to be expelled as feces through the rectum and anus.

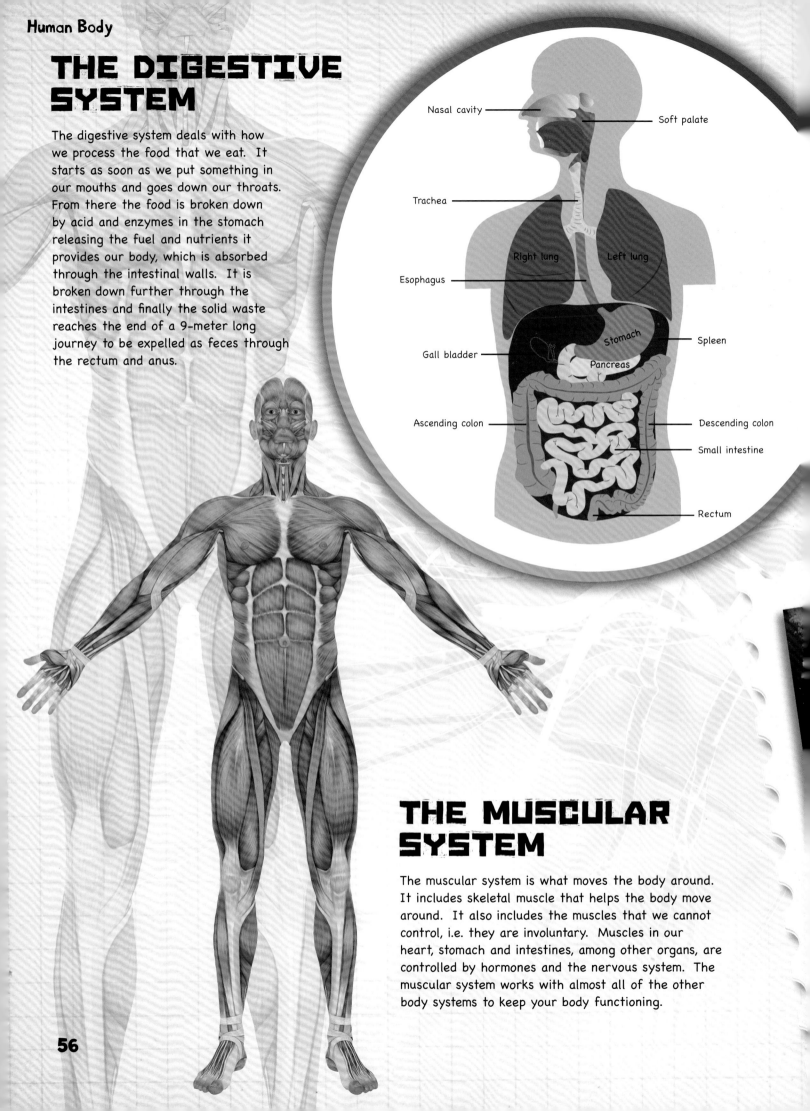

Nasal cavity

Soft palate

Trachea

Esophagus

Right lung

Left lung

Gall bladder

Stomach

Pancreas

Spleen

Ascending colon

Descending colon

Small intestine

Rectum

THE MUSCULAR SYSTEM

The muscular system is what moves the body around. It includes skeletal muscle that helps the body move around. It also includes the muscles that we cannot control, i.e. they are involuntary. Muscles in our heart, stomach and intestines, among other organs, are controlled by hormones and the nervous system. The muscular system works with almost all of the other body systems to keep your body functioning.

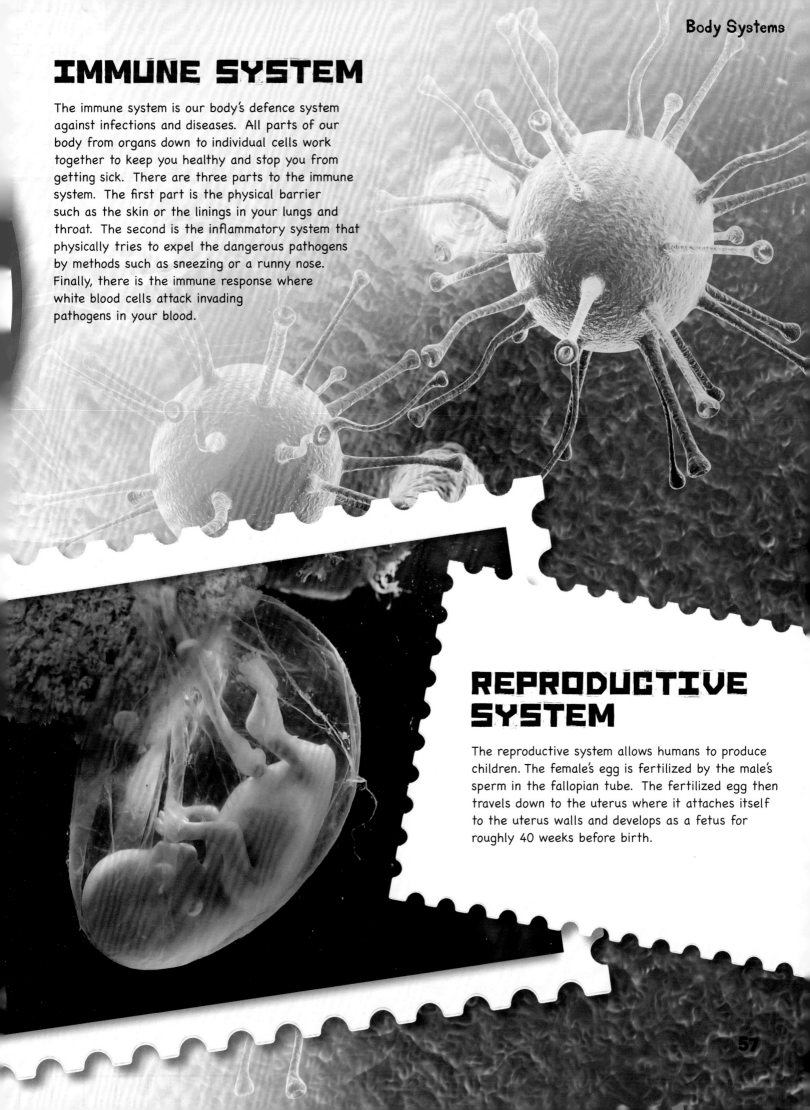

IMMUNE SYSTEM

The immune system is our body's defence system against infections and diseases. All parts of our body from organs down to individual cells work together to keep you healthy and stop you from getting sick. There are three parts to the immune system. The first part is the physical barrier such as the skin or the linings in your lungs and throat. The second is the inflammatory system that physically tries to expel the dangerous pathogens by methods such as sneezing or a runny nose. Finally, there is the immune response where white blood cells attack invading pathogens in your blood.

REPRODUCTIVE SYSTEM

The reproductive system allows humans to produce children. The female's egg is fertilized by the male's sperm in the fallopian tube. The fertilized egg then travels down to the uterus where it attaches itself to the uterus walls and develops as a fetus for roughly 40 weeks before birth.

MUSCULAR SYSTEM

Your muscular system contains more than 600 muscles and is the engine room of your body. Muscles are what make us move and keep us alive. They contract and relax as a result of electric pulses sent by the brain and central nervous system. This can be either voluntary, like going for a walk, but also involuntary meaning we have no control over it and we may not even notice it is happening. Your heart beating is a result of muscles contracting and relaxing and this is an example of an involuntary muscle in action.

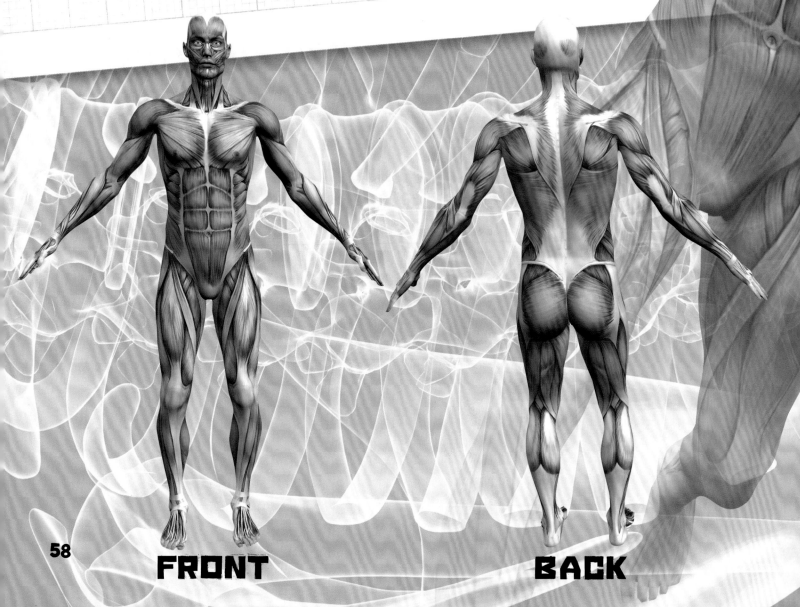

FRONT

BACK

Muscle

Fascia

Muscle fibers

Blood vessels

Sarcomere

Actin

Myofibril

Myosins

WHAT'S IT MADE OF?

Muscles are made from an elastic tissue that comes in fibers i.e. long strands. Each fiber is made up of smaller strands called myofibrils and these are made up of even smaller strands called myofilaments. These fibers are bunched into bundles call fascicles. The muscle contracts when the myofilaments slide past each other in response to nerve signals sent by the central nervous system. There are three types of muscle in the body, skeletal muscle, smooth muscle and cardiac muscle.

Skeletal muscle

Smooth muscle

Cardiac muscle

SKELETAL MUSCLE

Skeletal muscles are the ones most people think of when you say muscle. They make up the musculoskeletal system, which consists of your muscles and bones working together. Your skeletal muscles are bound to your joints and bones by tendons. Tendons are strong rope-like cords that link directly to the muscle and bones so that when the muscles contract or relax the movement also moves the bone and therefore whichever limb the bone is a part of. Muscles are positioned all around joints and limbs in complementary pairs so that one does the opposite of the other. This means that you can have full control of the movement.

59

FACE MUSCLES

Face muscles are funny because they are voluntary muscles that do not link directly to bone and are instead mostly attached to the skin. This allows us to pull all sorts of funny faces, raise an eyebrow and smile.

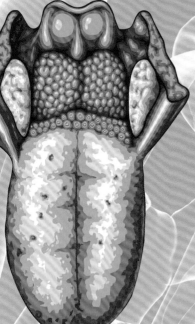

TONGUE TIED

Your tongue is actually a muscle that is only attached at one end. It is very strong, helps you to break down your food and eat. Of course it also helps us communicate and speak.

SMOOTH MUSCLES

Smooth muscle is an involuntary muscle meaning we have no control over using it. It is usually made up of layers of muscle one behind the other. Smooth muscle is all over your body. In the bladder, for example, there are muscles which allow you to hold in your urine (pee) when contracted. In your digestive system the smooth muscles contract and relax to move food down the intestines along its digestive journey or back up again when you vomit. You also have smooth muscles working at keeping your eyes focused.

MR HEARTZENEGGER I'LL BEAT BACK

Your heart is made of muscle called the cardiac muscle. It is also known as the myocardium. It is probably the most important muscle in the body as it pumps blood around your body. It is an involuntary muscle and works constantly with a special group of cells called pacemaker cells which control the heartbeat. Cardiac muscle is thick and strong. It contracts and relaxes making the heart beat around 60–100 times a minute, pumping blood around the body, providing oxygen and nutrients to all the living tissue.

Musculo-facto:

- You have all the muscle fiber you will ever have at birth. Once damaged they can't be replaced.
- Arnold Schwarzenegger has as many muscle fibers as you - They're just thicker!
- A single muscle cell of the sartorius muscle in the thigh can be more than 12 inches long.
- There are more than 600 voluntary muscles in the body.
- The strongest muscle of the body is the masseter muscle used for chewing!
- Your hand contains 20 different muscles.
- If all your muscles could pull in one direction you could create a force of 25 tons!
- Muscles account for approximately 40% of your body weight.
- It takes 17 muscles in your face to smile, but it takes 43 muscles to frown.
- You take approximately 5 million steps per year using your leg muscles!

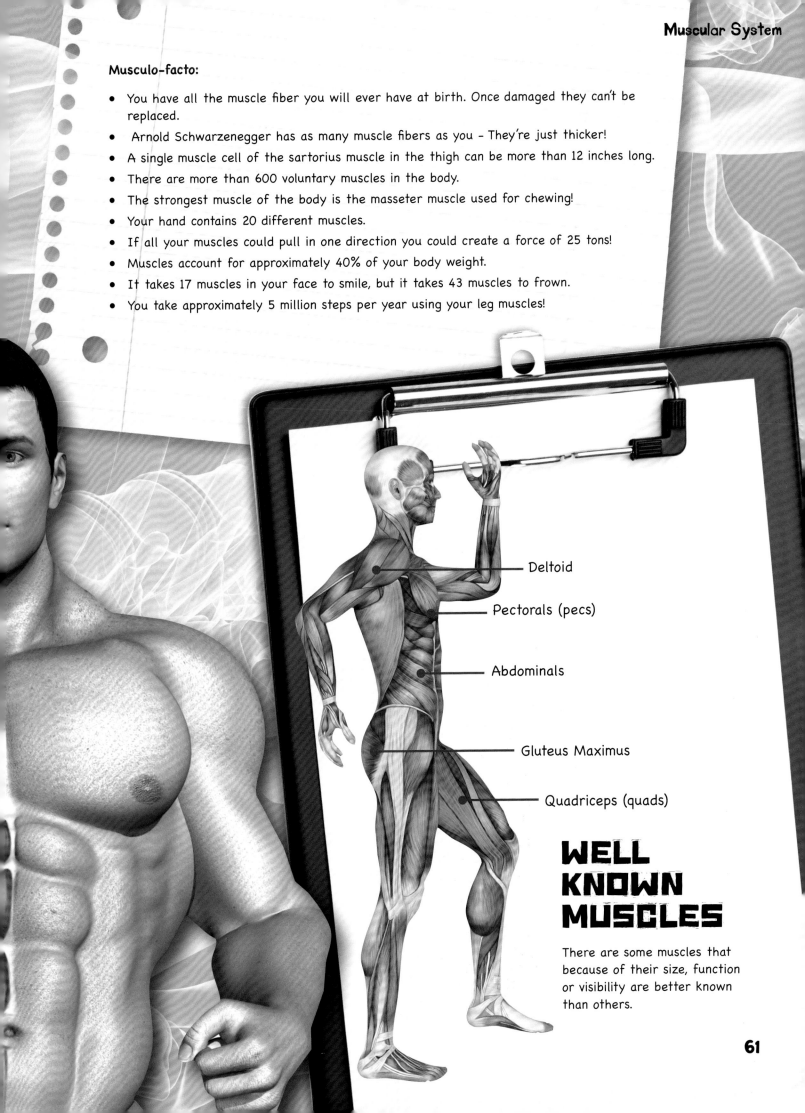

Deltoid

Pectorals (pecs)

Abdominals

Gluteus Maximus

Quadriceps (quads)

WELL KNOWN MUSCLES

There are some muscles that because of their size, function or visibility are better known than others.

SHOULDER COMPLEX

In mechanical terms, the shoulder is by far the most interesting part of the body. It is the most sophisticated and complicated joint in the body. The shoulder allows the arm to move in all directions, up and down, left and right, diagonally, in circles and more. If you think of the other major joints in the body, the elbow and knee are hinge joints allowing movement in one major direction, the ankle is also an amazing joint that allows for movement in many directions, but by far the greatest movement possible is from the shoulder.

HOW COOL!

The expression to 'carry the weight of the world on your shoulders' comes from a story in mythology. In Greek mythology, a Titan (an immortal being) called Atlas carried the weight of the world on his shoulders. This was a punishment given to him by Zeus, king of the gods.

This ingenious joint has allowed us to hunt, fight, use tools and play sports. Look at these pictures and imagine the movements the shoulder needs to make to perform these actions.

BOXING

ARCHERY

USING AN AX

PITCHING

PLAYING FOOTBALL

For the shoulder to allow so much different motion, the joint needs to be 'free' to move. This means that it should be unstable compared to other joints in the body, but there is a complex series of ligaments and muscles that keep it stable and in place.

63

HOW THE JOINTS WORK

The shoulder joins the bones of the humerus (the upper arm bone), the scapula (the shoulder blade) and the clavicle (the collar bone).

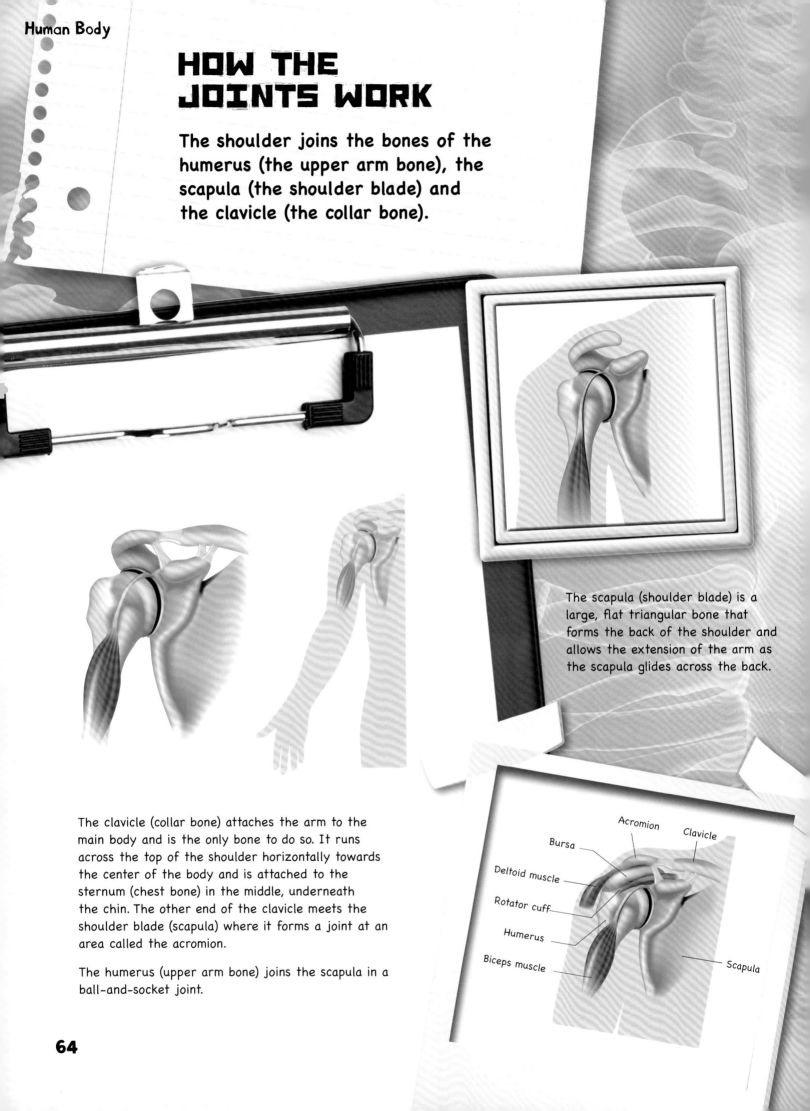

The scapula (shoulder blade) is a large, flat triangular bone that forms the back of the shoulder and allows the extension of the arm as the scapula glides across the back.

The clavicle (collar bone) attaches the arm to the main body and is the only bone to do so. It runs across the top of the shoulder horizontally towards the center of the body and is attached to the sternum (chest bone) in the middle, underneath the chin. The other end of the clavicle meets the shoulder blade (scapula) where it forms a joint at an area called the acromion.

The humerus (upper arm bone) joins the scapula in a ball-and-socket joint.

Acromion
Clavicle
Bursa
Deltoid muscle
Rotator cuff
Humerus
Biceps muscle
Scapula

AS EASY AS 1,2,3

There are three joints in the shoulder:

glenohumeral joint – This is also known as the shoulder joint and is the ball-and-socket joint where the ball end of the humerus bone fits into a socket in the shoulder blade. The socket is not very deep, which means that the arm is quite free to move and has amazing mobility. However this also means this joint is the easiest joint in the body to dislocate.

acromioclavicular joint – This is the joint between the collar bone and the top of the shoulder blade. It acts as a pivot joint and allows the arm to be raised above the head.

sternoclavicular joint – This is where the collar bone meets the sternum (chest bone).

ROPES AND SPRINGS

Holding all of the shoulder joints in place and linking them to muscles is a large number of complex ligaments and tendons. These 'ropes and springs' mean that the shoulder can perform a vast amount of motion without it falling apart. The ligaments are like ropes that tie the bones together and the tendons are like springs that link the muscles to the bones. This means the energy from the muscle can move the bones in the joint.

UPPER ARM

The upper arm links the shoulder to the elbow. There is just one bone in the upper arm called the humerus. This is also sometimes known as the 'funny bone'.

OUCH!!!

When you bang the back of you arm near the elbow you can receive a very strange and painful sensation right across your arm down to your hand. People often shout out 'Ouch I've hit my funny bone'. In fact they are not hitting a bone at all, instead they are hitting the not-very-well-protected nerve called the ulnar nerve.

HOW COOL!

THAT'S NOT THAT FUNNY!

So why is the humerus called the funny bone if it is the nerve you are hitting and not the bone? Some say that it is because humerus is close to humorous which means funny.

Others claim that it is because 'funny' can also mean a strange thing, and it certainly is a strange feeling you get if you hit your funny bone.

HA HA

MUSCLE MEN

Everyone knows about the two big muscles in the upper arm and people use this section of the body to show off how strong they are, even though these muscles are small in comparison to the legs and buttocks.

The biceps is the showing-off muscle in the middle of the arm.

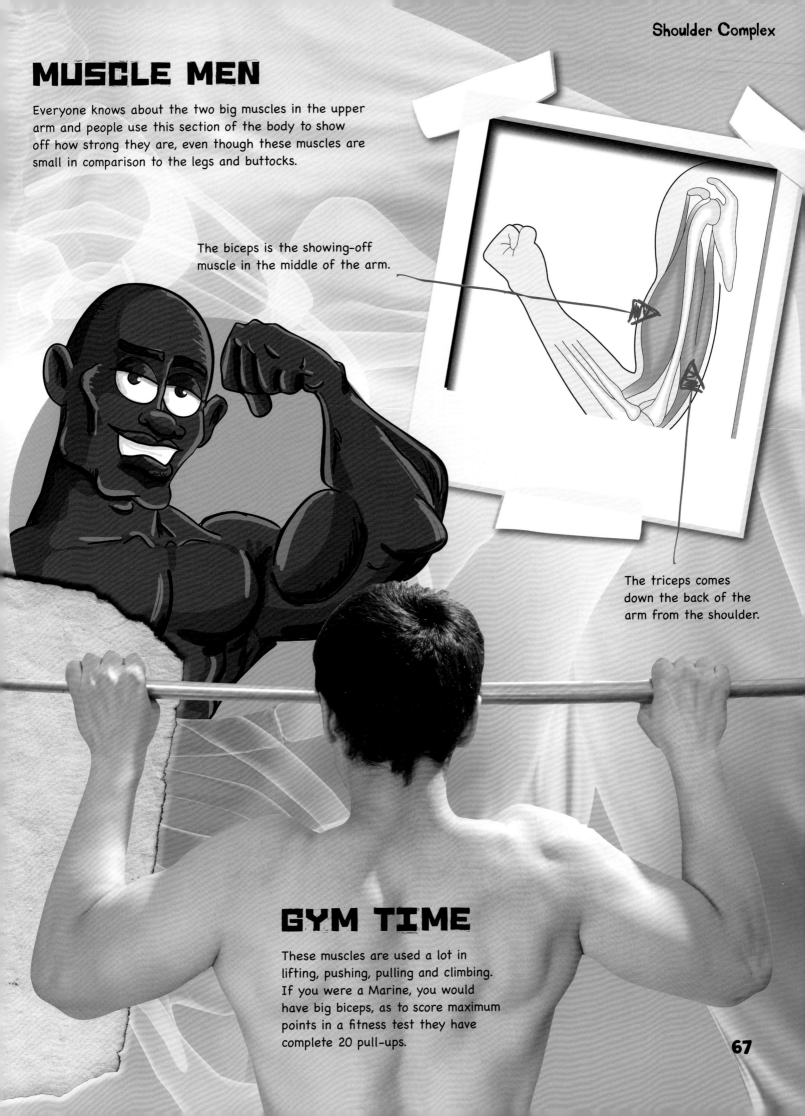

The triceps comes down the back of the arm from the shoulder.

GYM TIME

These muscles are used a lot in lifting, pushing, pulling and climbing. If you were a Marine, you would have big biceps, as to score maximum points in a fitness test they have complete 20 pull-ups.

67

ELBOW

The interesting elbow is the joint where the **humerus** (upper arm bone) meets the **radius** (lower arm bone) and **ulna** (lower arm bone). The elbow allows the arm to bend, which means we can move our arms a lot more and do a variety of things such as push-ups, scratching our head and perhaps most importantly, putting stuff in our mouths (or eating)!

SCAN ME
Instructions on page 5

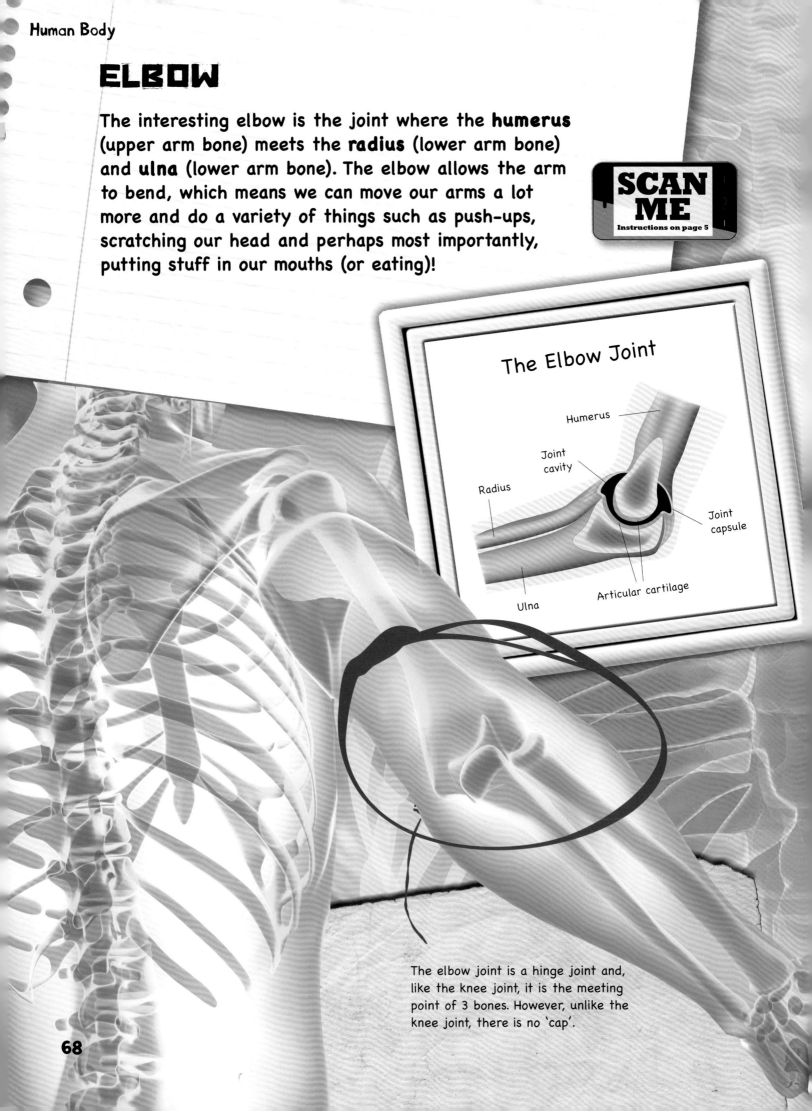

The Elbow Joint

Humerus

Joint cavity

Radius

Joint capsule

Articular cartilage

Ulna

The elbow joint is a hinge joint and, like the knee joint, it is the meeting point of 3 bones. However, unlike the knee joint, there is no 'cap'.

68

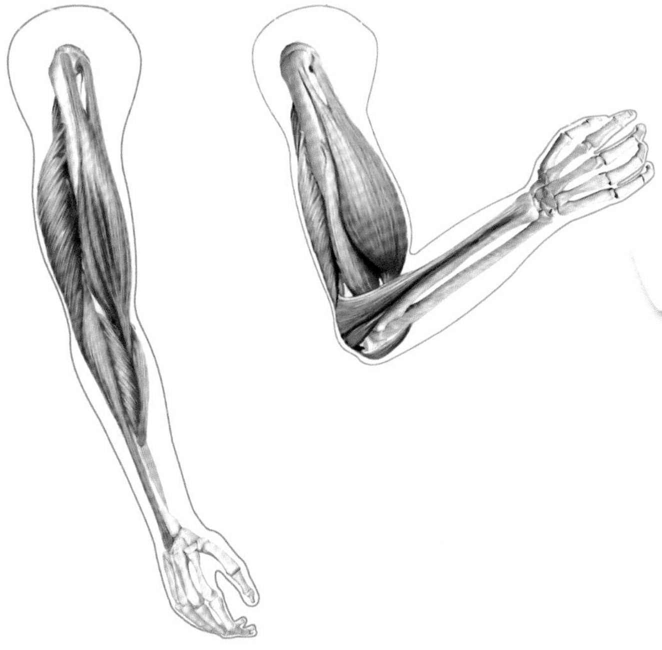

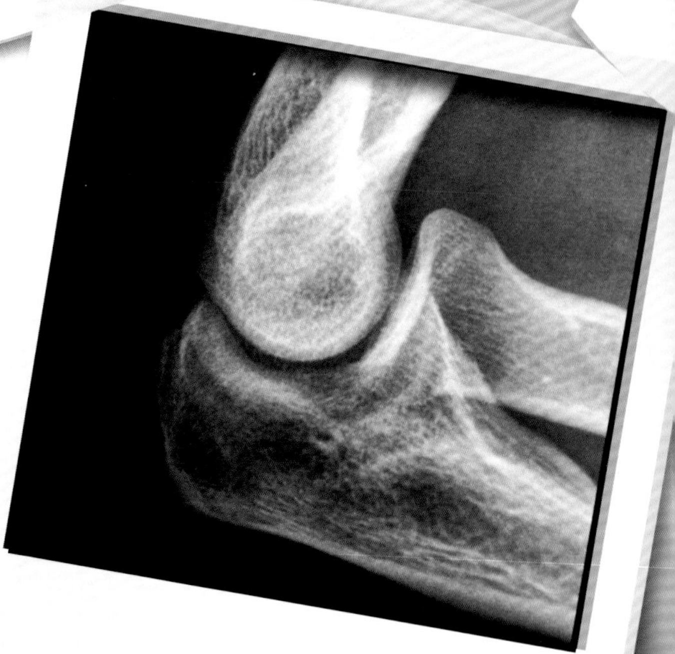

The elbow region has some recognizable areas like the elbow pit and the bony bit at the very tip of the elbow, which is called the olecranon.

ANYONE FOR A GAME OF TENNIS?

If you overuse your elbow, like those playing lots of tennis or golf, you can end up with tendonitis. Tendonitis means swelling up of tendons. Because tendonitis of the elbow is common among sportsmen and women who play tennis, it is also commonly known as tennis elbow.

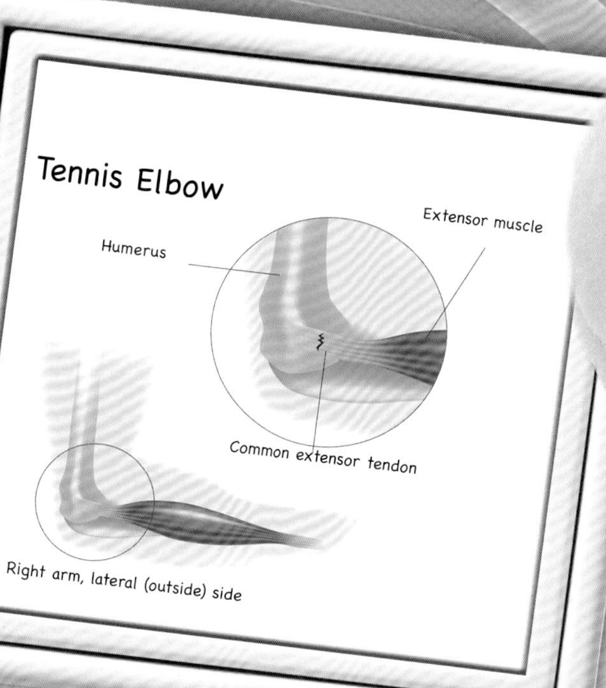

Tennis Elbow

Humerus

Extensor muscle

Common extensor tendon

Right arm, lateral (outside) side

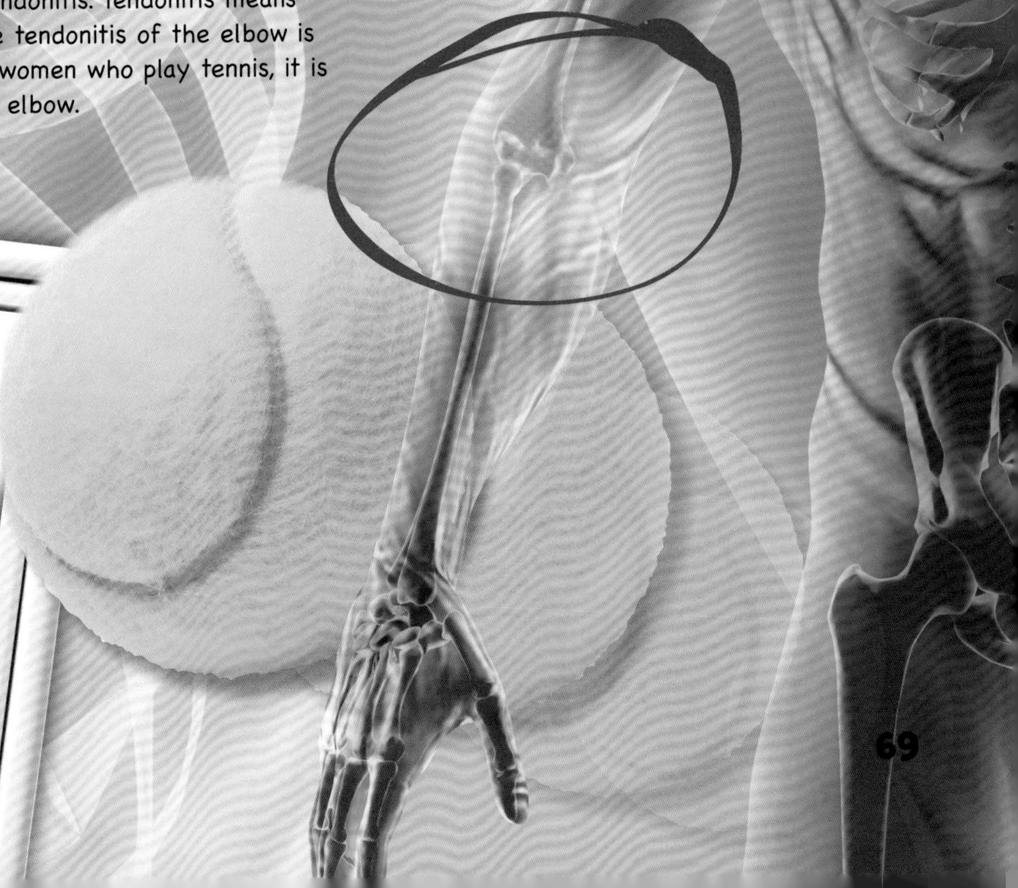

LOWER ARM

Coming from the elbow down to the wriggly wrist is the lower arm. This is also known as the **forearm**. Did you know that in anatomy, the 'arm' only refers to the upper arm between the shoulder and the elbow?

The forearm has two bones going down from the elbow all the way to the wrist. They are the **radius** and the **ulna**. As the forearm is often fallen on or used to try to break a fall, it is one of most commonly broken bones in the body.

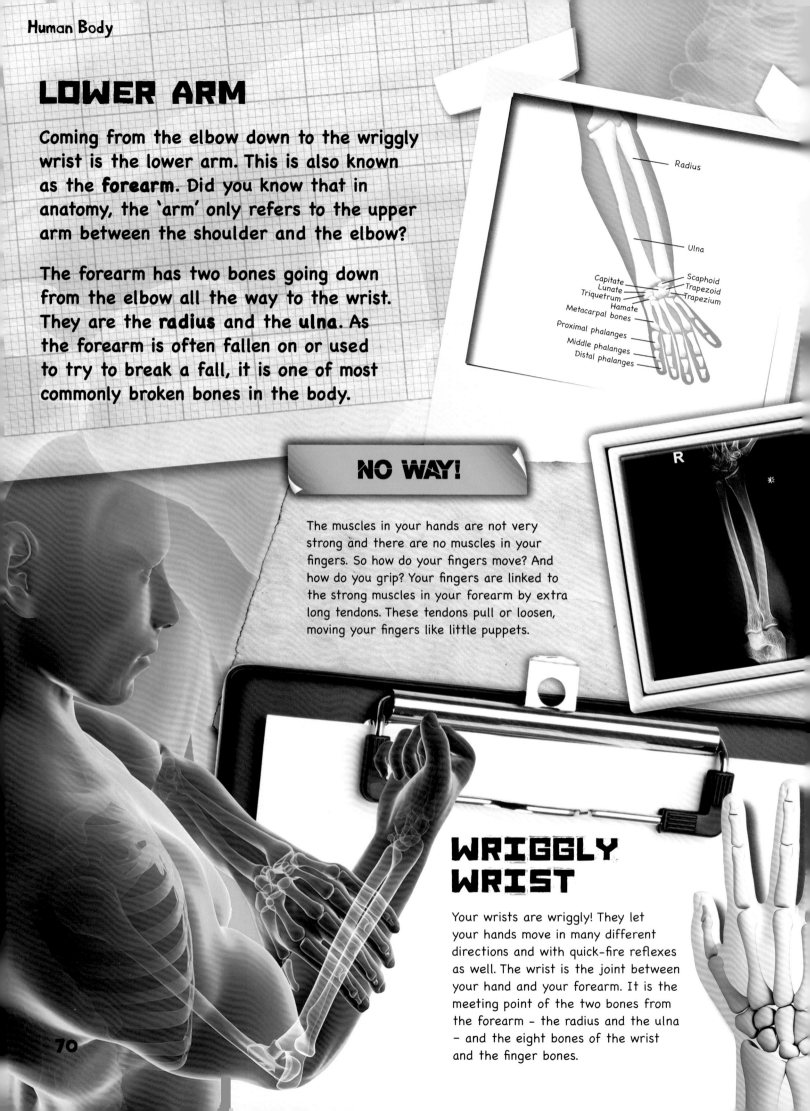

Radius

Ulna

Capitate
Lunate
Triquetrum
Hamate
Metacarpal bones
Scaphoid
Trapezoid
Trapezium
Proximal phalanges
Middle phalanges
Distal phalanges

NO WAY!

The muscles in your hands are not very strong and there are no muscles in your fingers. So how do your fingers move? And how do you grip? Your fingers are linked to the strong muscles in your forearm by extra long tendons. These tendons pull or loosen, moving your fingers like little puppets.

WRIGGLY WRIST

Your wrists are wriggly! They let your hands move in many different directions and with quick-fire reflexes as well. The wrist is the joint between your hand and your forearm. It is the meeting point of the two bones from the forearm - the radius and the ulna - and the eight bones of the wrist and the finger bones.

CARPAL BONES

There are eight bones in the wrist joint which link to the fingers on one side and the forearm bones on the other. These bones are called the carpal bones and are individually called: scaphoid, lunate, triquetral, pisiform, trapezium, trapezoid, capitate, hamate

GLUE AND PUPPET STRINGS

Holding all these bones together – eight carpal bones, two forearm bones and five finger bones – in such a small area is a complex array of ligaments. These ligaments act like a glue holding these bones and therefore the joint in place. When you have 'sprained your wrist' you have damaged one of these ligaments and it may take a while to repair itself.

Running through the complex array of ligaments are tendons from the muscles of the forearm linking with the five finger bones. These tendons act like puppet strings allowing us to move our fingers and grip things.

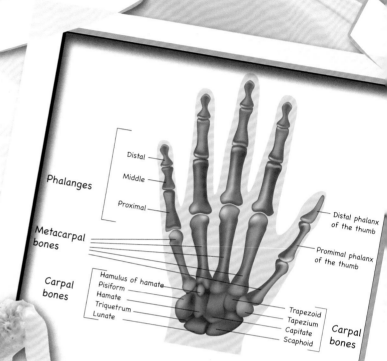

Phalanges
- Distal
- Middle
- Proximal

Metacarpal bones

Carpal bones

Hamulus of hamate
Pisiform
Hamate
Triquetrum
Lunate

Distal phalanx of the thumb

Promimal phalanx of the thumb

Trapezoid
Tapezium
Capitate
Scaphoid

Carpal bones

WRIST ACTIONS

WHAT CAN YOU DO WITH YOUR WRISTS?

CONDUCT

WAVE!

PLAY SQUASH

HANDS

Our hands are very special
because we are the only
animal that can use our
hands in a very complex way,
such as using tools, writing
and drawing or even using
a mobile phone!

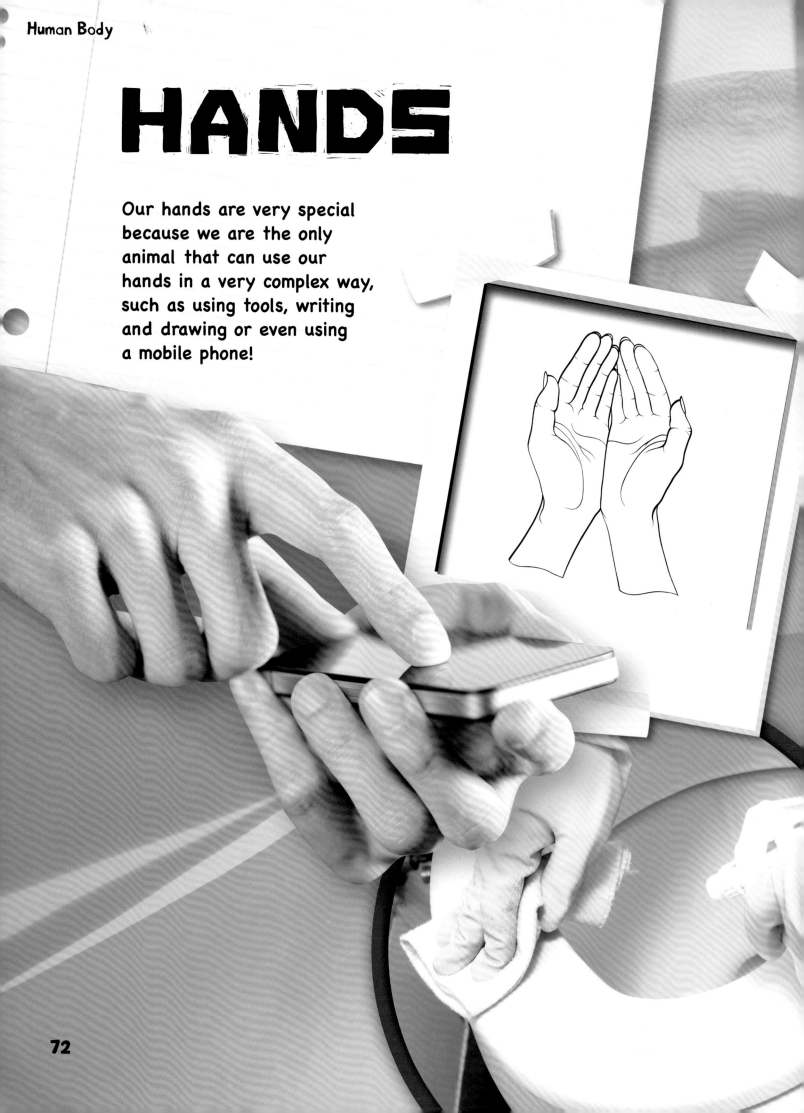

THUMBS UP

We all have hands that are mirror images of each other with one thumb and four fingers. Our thumbs are also free to move separately from the other fingers which allows us to grip items (try to pick up something without using your thumb, it's very difficult!). Thumbs like this are called **opposable thumbs**.

WASH YOUR HANDS

Think about all of the things you touched today. The telephone, door handles, the toilet seat, a sandwich. On all of the things you have touched today, you have come into contact with germs. So after your telephone call you went to the bathroom and after that you had lunch and ate a sandwich. Germs from everything you had touched were transported onto your sandwich and then into your mouth. Even worse, everyone who had touched the door handles and toilet seat would have transferred their germs to those items as well. You ate a germ sandwich! This is why it is important to wash your hands properly to eradicate potentially harmful germs before they can enter your body.

EWW, GROSS!

Filthy students – In a study, only 55% of female and 47% of male high-school students said they washed their hands after using the bathroom.

EWW, GROSS!

Just 21% of people wash their hands after handling money.

Most people like to pet an animal, but did you know that only 42% of people wash their hands after petting a dog or cat? These animals are dirtier than you think and often roll around the floor in feces and other animal's urine.

Only 32% of people wash their hands after coughing or sneezing. This means that when you shake their hand to say hello or goodbye, all of their germs are transferred to your hand! Gross!

COMMUNICATION

Some scientists say 70% of communication between people is body language rather than talking. The majority of that 70% communication would be **gesticulating**, moving your hands around, as you speak or even just to express yourself.

SIGN LANGUAGE

Isn't it cool to think that some people who are deaf (cannot hear) speak to other people through sign language. Below is American sign language, it varies from country to country just like speech does.

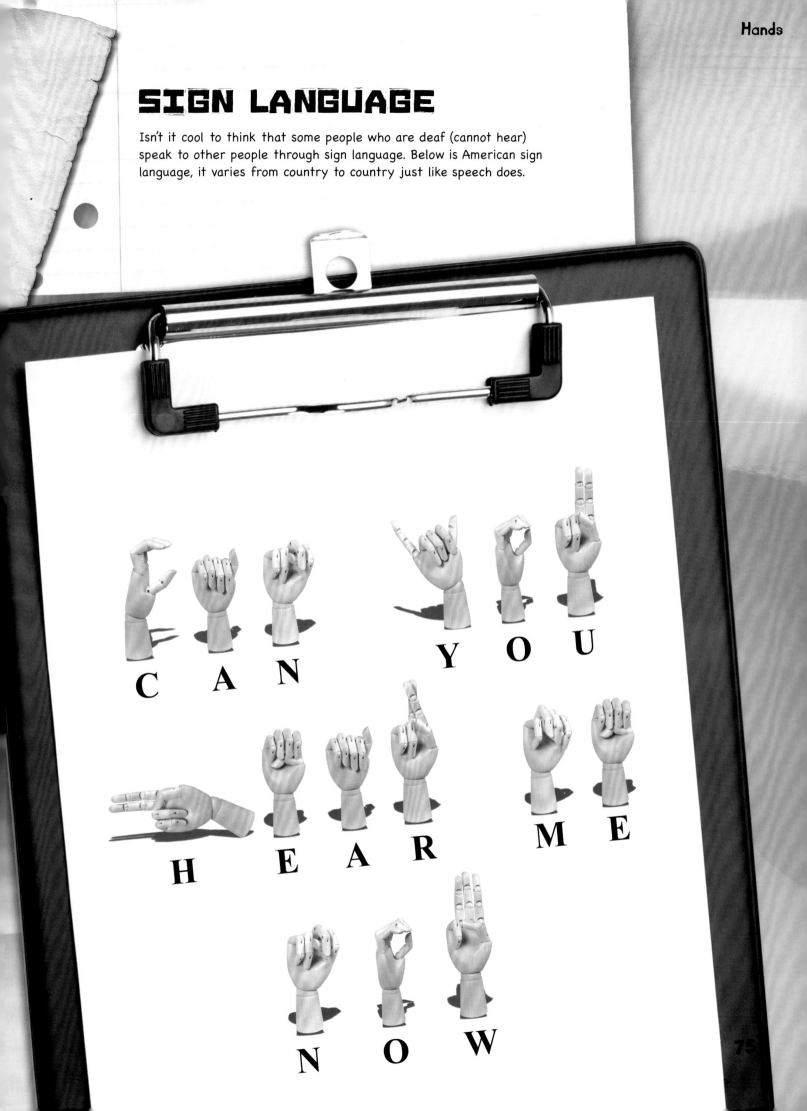

C A N

Y O U

H E A R

M E

N O W

THE HIP

The hip joint is one of the most important joints in the human body. It allows us to be very mobile and apart from the shoulder, it is the most flexible joint, allowing a great range of motion. Even so, it takes the weight of our body and the strong muscles of the hip and leg keep us upright and balanced.

The hip joint is a ball-and-socket joint formed between the hip-bone and the femur. The rounded head of the femur fits like a ball into the socket, a round cup-shaped structure in the hip joint. There is smooth cartilage lining this socket and the ball of the femur to allow moving bones to glide past each other. This cartilage also acts a flexible shock absorber preventing injury from heavy movement.

There are tough ligaments (connecting bones to bones) surrounding the hip joint keeping the bones in place. There are also many strong muscles and tendons (connecting muscles to bone) which hold the hip joint together and prevent dislocation.

BIONIC GRANDMA ROBO GRANDPA

Sometimes in old age the hip joint can wear out, or it can be broken in an accident. Surgeons can now replace it with a ball-and-socket joint made from metal and plastic which acts in the same way as the natural joint.

HIP MUSCLES

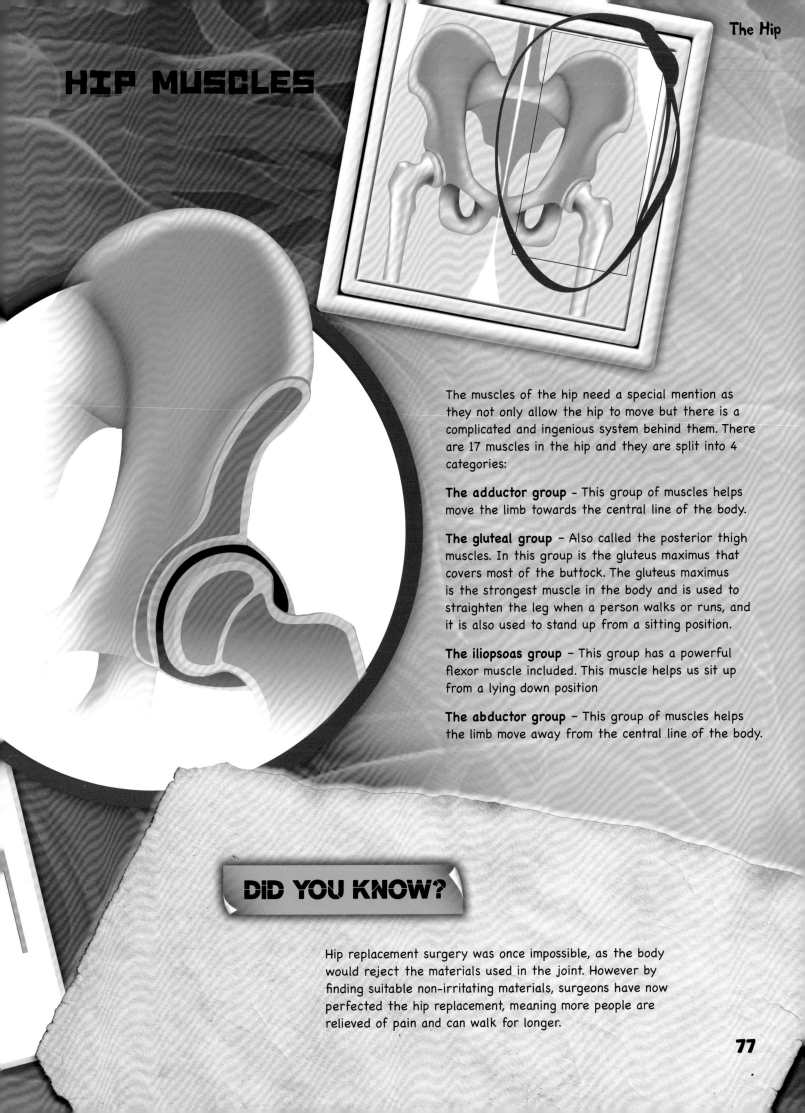

The muscles of the hip need a special mention as they not only allow the hip to move but there is a complicated and ingenious system behind them. There are 17 muscles in the hip and they are split into 4 categories:

The adductor group - This group of muscles helps move the limb towards the central line of the body.

The gluteal group – Also called the posterior thigh muscles. In this group is the gluteus maximus that covers most of the buttock. The gluteus maximus is the strongest muscle in the body and is used to straighten the leg when a person walks or runs, and it is also used to stand up from a sitting position.

The iliopsoas group – This group has a powerful flexor muscle included. This muscle helps us sit up from a lying down position

The abductor group – This group of muscles helps the limb move away from the central line of the body.

DID YOU KNOW?

Hip replacement surgery was once impossible, as the body would reject the materials used in the joint. However by finding suitable non-irritating materials, surgeons have now perfected the hip replacement, meaning more people are relieved of pain and can walk for longer.

LEGS

Legs are the wheels of the human body and what wheels they are! Powerful, strong and extremely useful, legs are used for getting us around, for running, jumping, playing sport and even sitting.

The legs start at the hip and buttocks where they join the pelvis, which connects them to the rest of the body. Going down from the hip you have the thigh, the real powerhouse of the leg. The thigh joins the lower leg at the knee joint, a very special and amazing part of your body. Your lower leg then meets the foot at the ankle.

SCAN ME
Instructions on page 5

SPORTS

We use our legs in all sorts of ways in sports. Here are some examples:

soccer – jumping, running, kicking the ball, tackling another player, blocking the ball

swimming – our legs are our propellers, powering us through the water

squash – we use our legs to lunge after the ball when it is hit low

golf – our legs keep our stance straight but we swing from our hips

EVOLUTION

As we evolved from apes and monkeys (primates), we moved from walking using four limbs to completely upright on our two legs (bipedal).

THIGH

The powerhouse of the legs, the thigh is the portion of the leg from the hip joint down to the knee joint.

There is one strong, large bone called the femur running down from the hip to the knee.

Surrounding this bone are some large and strong muscles which are split into three groups:

the anterior group - these muscles extend your legs and flex your thighs

the medial group - these muscles adduct and rotate your thigh

the posterior group - these muscles flex your leg and extend your thigh

DID YOU KNOW?

An elephant is the only land mammal that cannot jump – its bodyweight is simply too much for any joint to survive that impact.

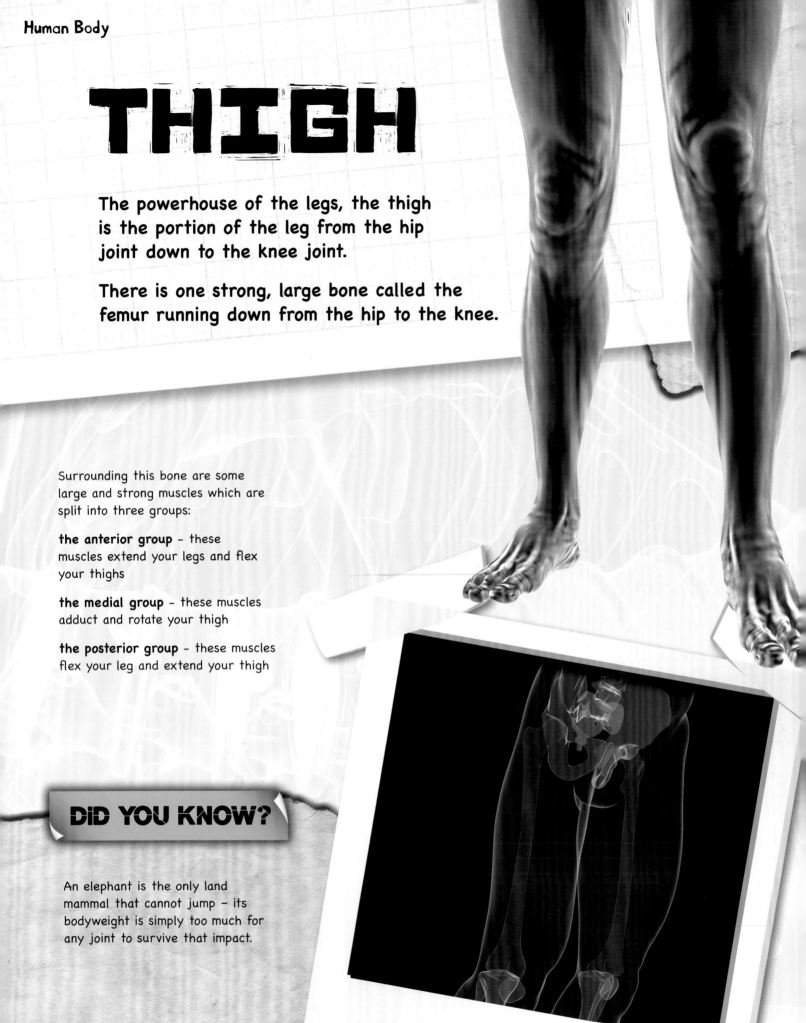

FUN FACT!

In 1836, Mexican General Santa Anna held an elaborate state funeral for his amputated leg.

AMAZING LEGS!

Our legs are truly amazing and allow us to run incredibly fast. Our top athletes have been getting the best out of our legs and over time they are improving dramatically. Look at the progression of the world records in 100m sprint since 1964.

Time	Athlete	Location of race	Date	Nationality
10.06	Bob Hayes	Tokyo, Japan	October 15, 1964	United States
10.03	Jim Hines	Sacramento, USA	June 20, 1968	United States
10.02	Charles Greene	Mexico City, Mexico	October 13, 1968	United States
9.95	Jim Hines	Mexico City, Mexico	October 14, 1968	United States
9.93	Calvin Smith	Colorado Springs, USA	July 3, 1983	United States
9.83	Ben Johnson	Rome, Italy	August 30, 1987	Canada
9.93	Carl Lewis	Rome, Italy	August 30, 1987	United States
9.92	Carl Lewis	Seoul, South Korea	September 24, 1988	United States
9.90	Leroy Burrell	New York, USA	June 14, 1991	United States
9.86	Carl Lewis	Tokyo, Japan	August 25, 1991	United States
9.85	Leroy Burrell	Lausanne, Switzerland	July 6, 1994	United States
9.84	Donovan Bailey	Atlanta, USA	July 27, 1996	Canada
9.79	Maurice Greene	Athens, Greece	June 16, 1999	United States
9.78	Tim Montgomery	Paris, France	September 14, 2002	United States
9.77	Asafa Powell	Athens, Greece	June 14, 2005	Jamaica
9.74	Asafa Powell	Rieti, Italy	September 9, 2007	Jamaica
9.72	Usain Bolt	New York, USA	May 31, 2008	Jamaica
9.69	Usain Bolt	Beijing, China	August 16, 2008	Jamaica
9.58	Usain Bolt	Berlin, Germany	August 16, 2009	Jamaica

KNEE

The knee is a fascinating joint and is very important because it supports all of our weight and is used in all of our horizontal (running, walking) and vertical (jumping, landing) movement. The knee is a hinge-type joint and can only bend one way.

The femur bone from the thigh meets the tibia and the fibula here at the knee joint. At the front of the knee there is another bone called the patella, also known as the knee cap. This triangle-shaped bone protects the junction of the tibia and femur where there are lots of tendons, ligaments and cartilage.

HOW COOL!

As at the hip joint, there is a complex group of ligaments that link the bones to each other. In particular, the most important of these ligaments are the ones that connect the femur to the tibia and the patella to the tibia.

FUN FACTS!

A lady from Russia called Svetlana Pankratova is thought to have the longest legs in the world at 132 cm.

The star of Riverdance Michael Flatley had his legs insured in 1999 for $40 million.

DID YOU KNOW?

There are also two main tendons in the knee: the quadriceps and the patella. Tendons are elastic tissue that connect muscle to the bone and the patella (knee cap) is held in place by these tendons.

To protect the bones from grinding against each other during movement, there is also fluid in the knee to keep the bones lubricated. There is also cartilage, which helps the bones pass over each other and also acts as a shock absorber.

LOWER LEG

The lower leg is made up of the tibia and the fibula bones, which go from the knee joint all the way down to the ankle.

Surrounding these two bones are strong muscles that are very useful for jumping and vertical motion. These include the calf muscles and the shin muscles.

The lower leg is often where soccer players have their legs broken. The shin is also very vulnerable to damage when playing a sport like soccer so the players tend to wear shin pads.

SCAN ME
Instructions on page 5

FUN FACTS

The body's longest muscle is the sartorius. It is a strap-like, narrow muscle that runs from the hip all the way to the knee.

Three months after an injury or fracture, the strength of an adult healing bone is already at 80% of normal.

Actors are often told 'to break a leg' before they go on stage. This is because of an old superstition in which it is bad luck to wish someone good luck, so you wish them bad luck instead – to break a leg!

BROKEN BONES

Most broken bones happen in the upper body: the wrist, the forearm and above the elbow. This is because when we fall, it's a natural instinct for us to throw our hands out in an attempt to stop the fall. However, arguably the most painful and serious fractures occur in the legs.

There are many different types of fractures. When the break is incomplete and doesn't go through the whole bone, it is called an incomplete fracture. Two types of incomplete fracture are:

torus fracture – this is where one side of the bone bends, raising a little bump, without breaking the other side

greenstick fracture – this is where one side of the bone is broken and the other side bends. It is called a greenstick fracture because it resembles the break you would get if you tried to break a green stick.

Mature bones are more likely to break completely as they are less bendy. These breaks are called a complete fracture and may be one of these types:

closed fracture – this is where the broken bone does not break the skin.

compound fracture – this is a fracture where one of the ends of the broken bone breaks through the skin.

hairline fracture – this is where the bone is not displaced but there is a thin crack straight through the bone.

comminuted fracture – this is a nasty break where the bone is broken into more than two pieces or crushed.

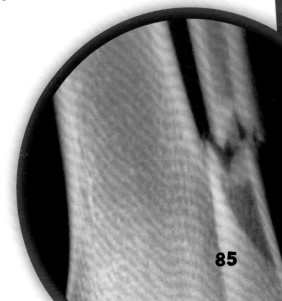

ANKLE

The ankle is the junction that connects your foot to your leg. It is very important in allowing humans to be mobile. Thanks to our amazing ankles we can walk, jump, run, dance and play sport.

Our ankles are made up of 3 major bones that all meet at the top of your foot where it meets your leg. At this point the main bones of the lower leg meet with the foot and are all connected by strong but flexible ligaments.

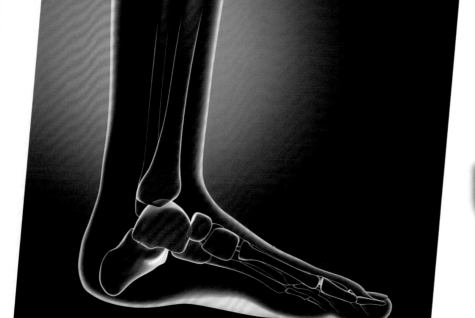

DID YOU KNOW?

An ankle sprain is one of the most common sports injuries. Be careful out there!

BONE GRINDING

As the bones all meet at the ankle joint and are connected together by ligaments we have a shiny, smooth material called **cartilage** at the end of the bones to protect them from grinding together.

The Ankle Joint of the Right Foot

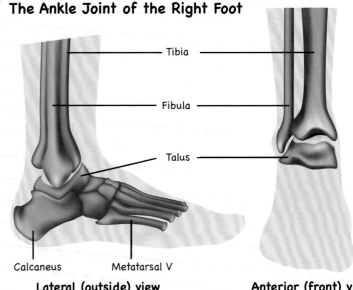

Tibia

Fibula

Talus

Calcaneus

Metatarsal V

Lateral (outside) view

Anterior (front) view

ROPES

All over the body, but especially useful in the ankle, we have strong ligaments which connect bones together as if they were tied with ropes. These ligaments linking the bones together keep the bones in place. Sometimes we can injure these ligaments, such as when you **sprain your ankle.**

Ankle Sprains

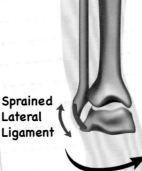
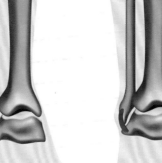
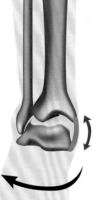

Sprained Lateral Ligament

Sprained Medial Ligament

Inversion

Normal

Eversion

PULLEYS

So that we can run and jump, we need strong muscles to **contract** and **relax** like a series of pulleys working to move your body. However, these muscles need to be connected to the bone so we can use the energy created. We have special links between bones and muscles all over the body which are called **tendons**. One of the most useful and important tendons in your body is the **Achilles tendon**, which is found in the ankle.

SUPER FACT!

Every time you take a step, walk, run or jump, you use your Achilles tendons. Make sure you're wearing the correct shoes for sport so that you don't damage them.

ACHILLES TENDON

The Achilles tendon in the ankle is named after Achilles from Greek mythology. It was predicted that Achilles would die young, so when he was a baby his mother travelled to a mythical river and dipped him in it, holding on to him by his heel. This made Achilles invulnerable (which meant that he could not be killed) except for his heel, which had not been washed in the magical waters. Achilles grew up to fight many epic battles and he was considered a strong and mighty warrior because he was invincible. However, in his last battle he was shot through the heel by a poisoned arrow. This was the one part of him that was vulnerable and so he died.

ACHILLES HEEL

Saying someone has an Achilles heel is identifying their major point of weakness in spite of their overall strength.

A common and painful sports injury is a broken Achilles tendon. When this snaps it makes a loud noise and a sportsperson will immediately know they will be out of action for a long time. Kobe Bryant, star of the NBA's LA Lakers, snapped his Achilles tendon in April 2013 in what could have been a career-ending injury.

HOW COOL!

If you injure your ankle when doing sport, make sure you put something ice cold on it. This will help prevent swelling and pain.

FEET

Like our hands, our feet are also very important parts of our body. They allow us to walk and run, jump and land. We use our feet more for sport now, but as we evolved our feet were critical to our survival. They enabled us to chase other animals for food and spread humanity across the world to every part of the globe.

USEFUL FACT

We all have a big toe and 4 smaller toes each providing useful balance when standing.

HOW COOL!

BONY FEET

Over 25% of all the bones in your entire body are in your feet.

Baby Child Teen Adult

DID YOU KNOW?

WHAT A HIKE!

The average person takes 10,000 steps a day. That's about 115,000 miles in a lifetime, enough to circle the world 4 times!

SWEATY FEET

Did you know that there are over 250,000 sweat glands on a pair of feet? They produce up to half a pint of moisture a day.

WALKING WOMEN

The average woman walks 3 miles more per day than the average man.

ROYAL SHOE SIZES

Shoe sizes were invented in England by King Edward II in 1324. He declared that one shoe size should be the diameter of one barleycorn – a third of an inch – and this is still used today.

HUMAN SKELETAL SYSTEM

Without organs, muscles and skin, all that is left are bones and like most animals the Human body contains a framework of bones. When joined together, these bones are called a Skeleton. This Skeleton provides the perfect structure for our organs, muscles and skin and gives protection to our insides. It also helps us to walk, run and move.

Each bone within the Human Skeleton is important, and all are specially adapted to best perform their role within the body.

DID YOU KNOW?

Without your skeleton you would be a blobby mass of organs that would have no structure or shape. The skeleton gives our bodies their shape and movement.

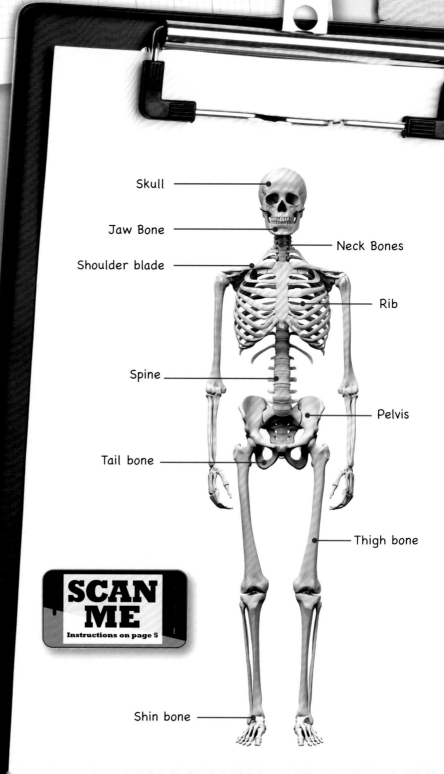

Skull

Jaw Bone

Neck Bones

Shoulder blade

Rib

Spine

Pelvis

Tail bone

Thigh bone

SCAN ME
Instructions on page 5

Shin bone

DID YOU KNOW?

There are 206 separate bones in an adult human skeleton. Most of these, over 50%, are in the Hands and Feet, two parts of our body which perform the most complicated movements.

The Skeleton is not unique to Humans and in fact most animals have a skeletal backbone (spine) and are called vertebrates. Animals that do not have a spine are called invertebrates.

The backbone has 26 bones stacked on top of one another vertically. 24 of these bones are known as vertebrae, and the remaining 2 are actually made of four or five vertebrae fused together. In between each vertebrae there is a soft pad of cartilage which acts as a cushion to stop each vertebra bone banging and rubbing against other, which would wear the bones out.

Cervical vertebrae

Thoracic vertebrae

Lumbar vertebrae

Sacral vertebrae

AND THE WINNER IS...

The biggest bone in the human body is in the leg. It is called the femur, or thighbone. Most people's femur, when measured, works out to be about a quarter of their height.

Adult humans have 206 bones within their skeletal system – but on the day we are born we are born with between 270 and 350 bones in our newborn body. These extra bones actually join together, called 'fusing', as the body grows over time.

YOU'RE KIDDING ME

You are taller in the morning when you wake up than if you measured yourself when you got home from school! No kidding, This is because the activities performed by us during the day make the discs between the back vertebrae compress. Gravity causes this and reduces your height during the day, but at night, the discs go back to normal when we sleep and so we gain about half an inch in height for the morning.

OUR CLOSEST RELATIVE

The skeletons of Chimpanzees and humans are very similar and point to them both evolving from the same ancestor. However, there are a number of differences as well. Chimps have smaller brains than humans so their brainbox skull is smaller. Unlike humans they also have a long, pointy jaw. But did you know the human DNA has a 97% similarity to Chimp DNA!

AMAZING!

The skeleton makes up 14% of an adult human's total body weight.

SING AND LEARN

CHORUS

Oh those bones, oh those bones,
oh those skeleton bones.
Oh those bones, oh those bones,
oh those skeleton bones.
Oh those bones, oh those bones,
oh those skeleton bones.
Oh mercy how they scare!

VERSE 1

With the toe bone connected
to the foot bone,
and the foot bone connected
to the ankle bone,
and the ankle bone connected
to the leg bone.
Oh mercy how they scare!

VERSE 2

With the leg bone connected
to the knee bone,
and the knee bone connected
to the thigh bone,
and the thigh bone connected
to the hip bone.
Oh mercy how they scare!

VERSE 3

With the hip bone connected
to the back bone,
and the back bone connected
to the neck bone,
and the neck bone connected
to the head bone,
Oh mercy how they scare!

VERSE 4

With the finger bone connected
to the hand bone,
and the hand bone connected
to the arm bone,
and the arm bone connected
to the shoulder bone,
Oh mercy how they scare!

VERSE 5

With the shoulder bone connected
to the back bone,
and the back bone connected
to the neck bone,
and the neck bone connected
to the head bone.
Oh mercy how they scare!

95

BONES

When you think of bones do you think of Halloween and all the skeleton costumes running around outside 'trick or treating'? Or do you think of dogs in the back yard digging a hole to hide their latest catch. Either way we are all made of bones and our skeleton is a fascinating thing. It will outlast us so that after we die our bones will survive for many years to come. Bones truly are bonkers, they not only form the shape of our body but they protect our vital organs.

HOW CAN YOU LOSE YOUR BONES?

When you are an adult you have 206 individual bones. However, when you were young you had more! Many of these bones fused together to form stronger bones covering a larger area to protect the body.

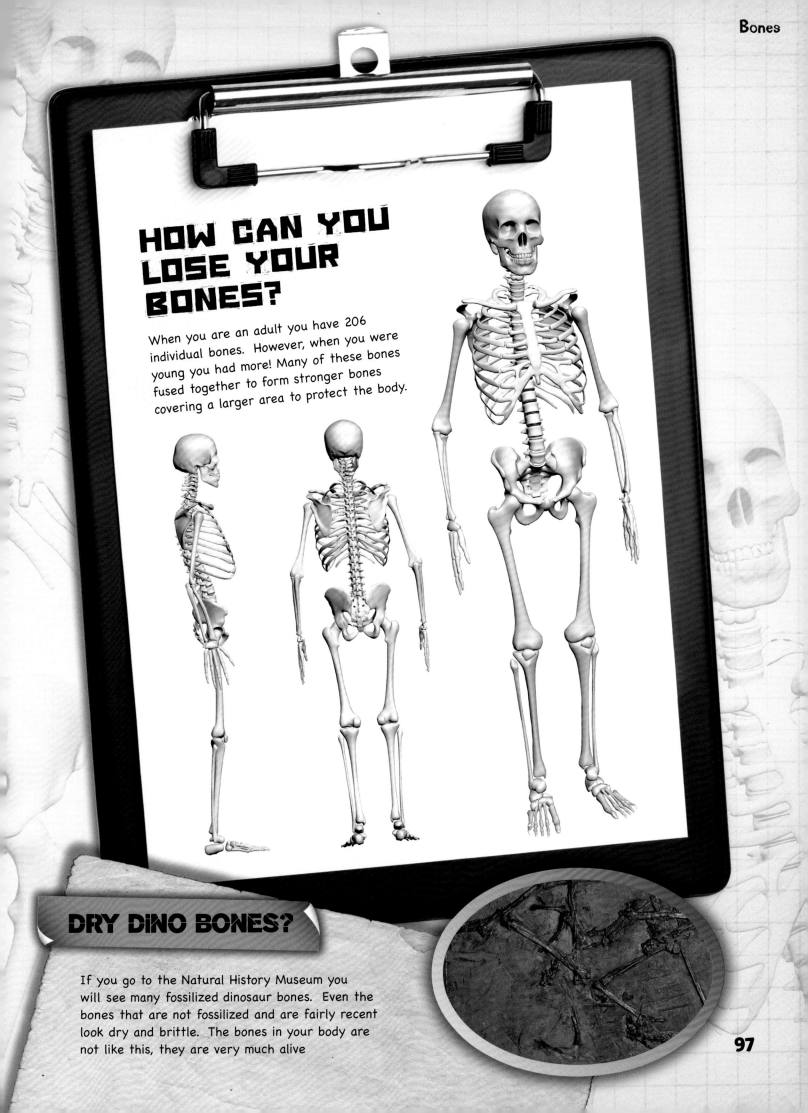

DRY DINO BONES?

If you go to the Natural History Museum you will see many fossilized dinosaur bones. Even the bones that are not fossilized and are fairly recent look dry and brittle. The bones in your body are not like this, they are very much alive

spongy bone

compact bone

bone marrow

THEY'RE ALIVE THEY'RE ALIVE!

Your bones are alive and constantly change and even grow. They have three main parts, the **compacted** section, the **spongy** section and the **bone marrow**.

Compact
This part of the bone is the hardest and as the name suggests is compacted. It is made out of calcium, which we get from our food. When we are growing up one of the main sources of calcium we get is from milk, which is why moms say to drink your milk 'to help your bones grow'.

Spongy
Underneath the compact (protective) layer there is the spongy part of the bone. The spongy part is also called the **cancellous**. This section has a honeycomb structure with many spaces that means it makes the bone lighter but it is still very strong.

Marrow
Bone marrow has a jelly-like texture and is present in most of the bones in the body. Apart from helping form the structure of your body, the bone marrow produces necessary red blood cells at an incredible rate, 3 million cells per second!

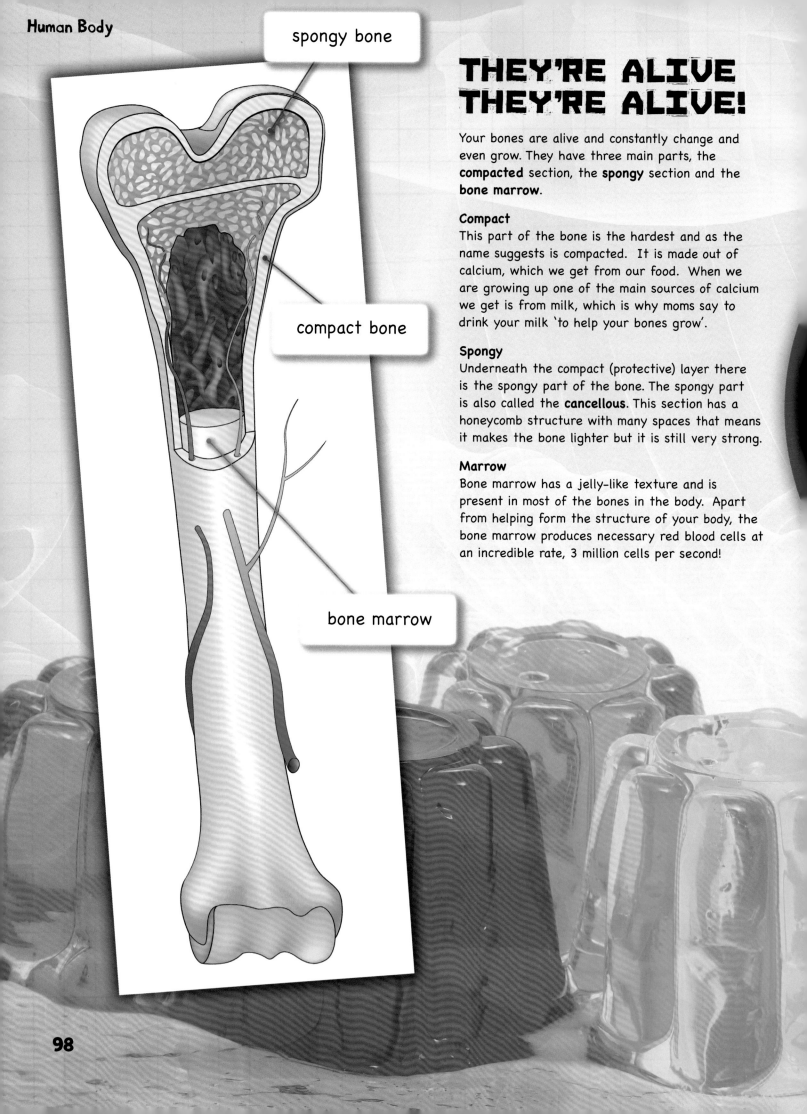

GROWING BONES

When you were born you had over 300 bones. These fuse together over time to leave 206 bones as an adult. Some of the bones you are born with are made of cartilage and other bones partly made up of cartilage. Cartilage is soft and flexible. Most of this cartilage is replaced by bone made of calcium over the years as you grow. When you reach the age of 25 this process is complete and your bones will not grow any further.

FUN BONY FACTS:

- The smallest bone is in the ear. It is called the stirrup bone and is the size of half a grain of rice.

- The biggest bone is in the leg. It is called the femur or thighbone.

- A broken bone will take about 2.5 months to heal.

- The strongest bone in the skeleton is the jawbone.

- Over half the bones in the skeleton are found in the hands and feet. The hand alone has 27 bones - in each one.

99

SPINE

Your spine is also known as your backbone and is a strong yet flexible column of ring-like bones called **vertebrae**. It starts at the skull and runs down the middle of your back all the way to your pelvis. It is S-shaped, has a hollow cavity in the middle and is very flexible. This strength and flexibility allows you to hold your head and body upright, while the cavity in the center of the vertebrae is a protective channel for the incredibly important but very delicate spinal cord.

VERTEBRAE

There are 33 vertebrae (bones) in your spine. Each is shaped with a hole in the middle so that your delicate spinal cord can run through it. In between your vertebrae are shock absorbers. These are pads of tough, fibrous cartilage that cushion your vertebrae and absorb shock. They are called **intervertebral discs** and together with the S-shape of your spine, they prevent shock and pain in your head when you walk or run. Although the joints between individual vertebrae are not very flexible, by working together as a whole, the spine provides a wide range of movement. You can arch backwards, bend forwards and twist from side to side as the spinal column works together with the strong ligaments and muscles in your back and around the vertebrae to stabilize your spine and control the movement.

You can divide the spine into five different regions, starting at the top:

cervical vertebrae – at the top there are seven cervical vertebrae that allow you to nod and shake your head. These are also the main supports of your head and neck.

thoracic vertebrae – the next 12 vertebrae are called the thoracic vertebrae and they are attached to your ribs.

lumbar vertebrae – there are five lumbar vertebrae below the thoracic vertebrae. These five vertebrae carry most of the weight of your upper body.

sacrum – moving into the pelvis area, there are five vertebrae fused together called the sacrum. This makes up the back wall of your pelvis.

coccyx – right at the end of your spine is the coccyx, which is made up of four fused vertebrae. This is the evolutionary remains of what used to be your tail.

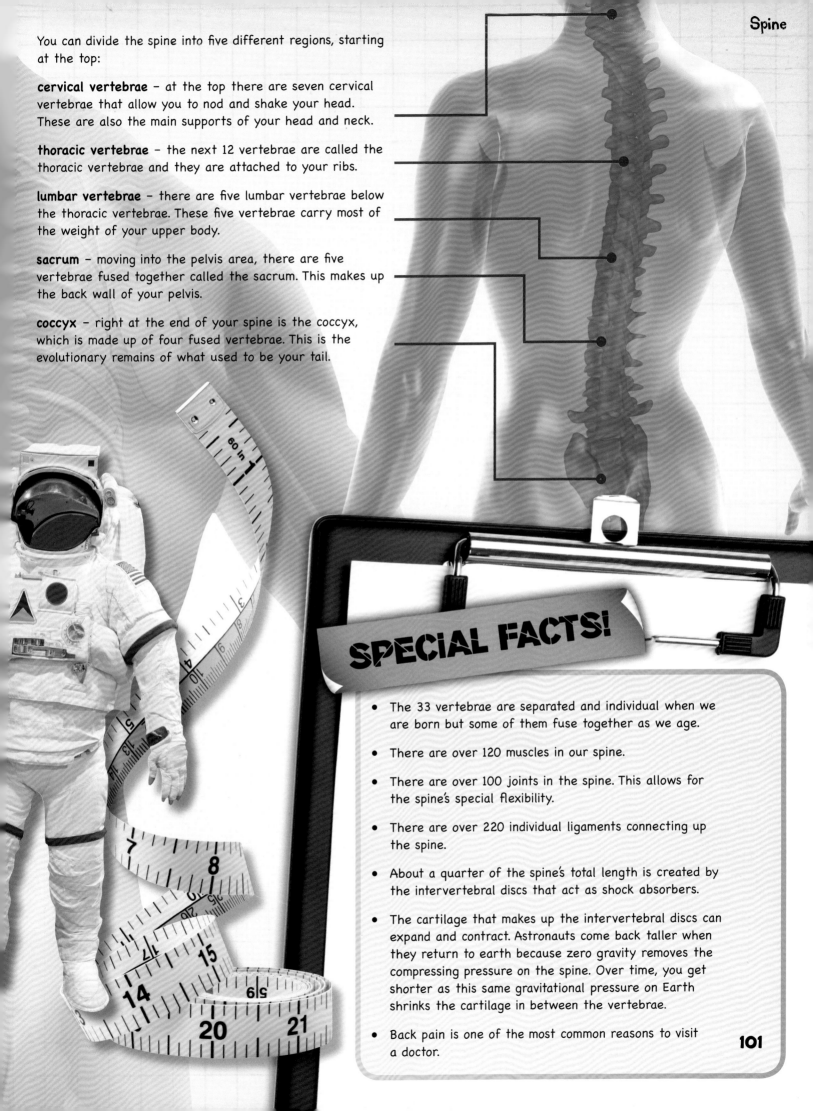

SPECIAL FACTS!

- The 33 vertebrae are separated and individual when we are born but some of them fuse together as we age.

- There are over 120 muscles in our spine.

- There are over 100 joints in the spine. This allows for the spine's special flexibility.

- There are over 220 individual ligaments connecting up the spine.

- About a quarter of the spine's total length is created by the intervertebral discs that act as shock absorbers.

- The cartilage that makes up the intervertebral discs can expand and contract. Astronauts come back taller when they return to earth because zero gravity removes the compressing pressure on the spine. Over time, you get shorter as this same gravitational pressure on Earth shrinks the cartilage in between the vertebrae.

- Back pain is one of the most common reasons to visit a doctor.

101

THE LIVER

The liver is the largest organ inside our bodies and is very important because you can't live without it. The liver is found in the abdomen underneath the diaphragm, inside your ribcage. When you are fully grown, your liver will be around the size of a football and weigh 3.1 pounds or 1.4 kg.

The liver is a bit like a chemical factory, receiving nutrients that it either stores or converts and sends off to other parts of the body.

The liver performs over 500 functions but its three main jobs are:

1. Cleaning your blood.

2. Producing an important liquid called **bile** used for digestion.

3. Storing energy that is a form of a sugar called glycogen.

CLEANING THE BLOOD

The liver cleans the blood by taking out toxins or poisons that have come from the body's normal processes or from the foods we eat. It sorts out the good nutrients and sends these to the parts of the body that need them. The remaining bad stuff or waste our bodies don't need is then carried by bile back into the intestine. It is then expelled from our bodies when we poop or is sent to the kidneys for an extra clean and comes out as pee.

MAKING BILE

Bile is a thick greenish-brown digestive juice produced by the liver. Bile is stored in the gallbladder until the body needs it. Bile contains wastes and broken down blood cells from the liver. When it is needed, it travels along the bile duct into the duodenum, where special bile salts breakdown the fats into tiny droplets so they can be absorbed into the bloodstream.

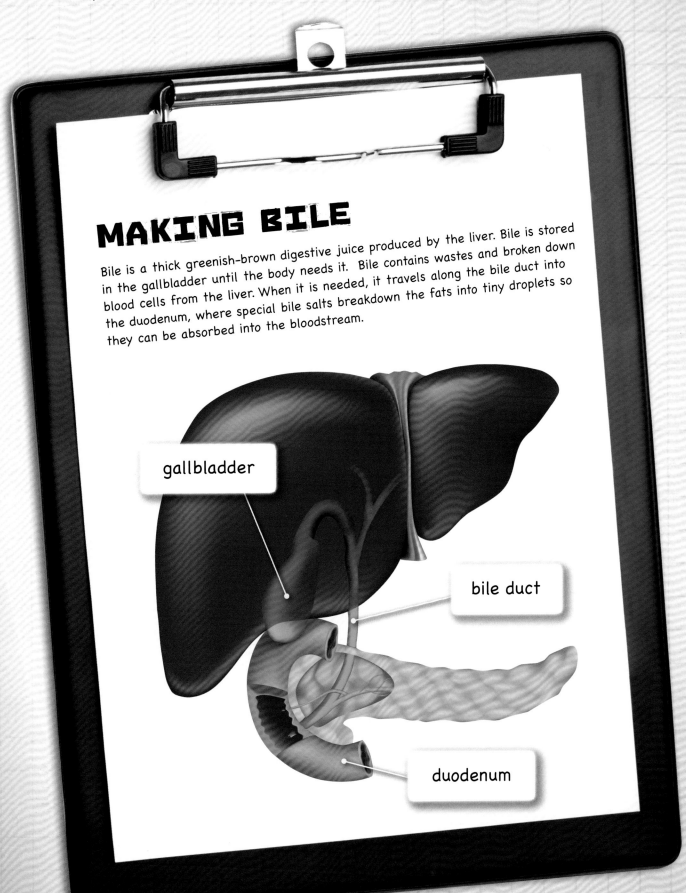

gallbladder

bile duct

duodenum

STORING ENERGY

The liver is also a bit like a reserve fuel tank. When the body breaks down carbohydrates which are found in foods such as bread, fruit and milk, they are turned into a type of sugar called **glucose**. Glucose is used by our cells as fuel. The liver stores glucose for us in the form of glycogen and releases it into the blood stream when the body needs a quick energy boost, or when the body's glucose levels have dropped.

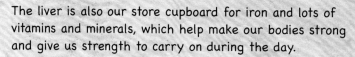

COOL FACTS ABOUT OUR LIVER!

The liver is also our store cupboard for iron and lots of vitamins and minerals, which help make our bodies strong and give us strength to carry on during the day.

The liver helps your blood clot and stops you bleeding to death! The liver produces two substances called fibrinogen and prothrombin which, when combined with platelets in the blood, produce a sticky glob that clots the blood and stops you bleeding.

The liver fights and destroys germs. The liver contains over half of our body's macrophages, a form of germ-killing white blood cell. These clever cells weaken and destroy bacteria and fight infection.

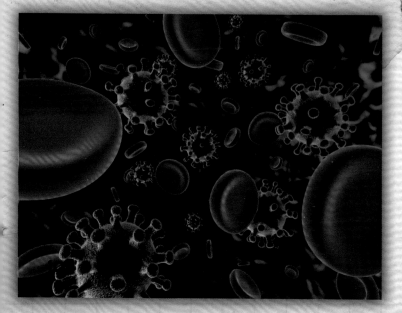

FUN FACT

Our liver looks a bit like an eggplant. Eggplants are very good for the liver, as they may slow the progression of fatty liver disease when you eat them as part of a healthy diet. Other foods that are good for your liver include garlic, grapefruit and leafy green vegetables.

THE LIVER IS AWESOME

Next time you take some medicine, think about your liver! Our clever liver takes out the active ingredients from medicine and breaks them down so our bodies can use them.

DISEASES OF THE LIVER

There are over 100 types of liver disease, caused by a variety of factors and affecting everyone from infants to older adults. The most common causes of liver disease are viral hepatitis, obesity and alcohol and drug use.

HOW DO WE LOOK AFTER THIS AMAZING ORGAN?

Living healthily is the best way to care for your liver. The liver is easily damaged by too much alcohol or if a person is very overweight. So be active, eat a healthy diet and remember we can't live without our livers!

CARDIOVASCULAR SYSTEM

The cardiovascular system is the system that carries (or circulates) blood through arteries, veins, blood vessels and capillaries to all parts of our body. The heart is central to the cardiovascular system. Its main function is to pump blood around the body.

THERE ARE ACTUALLY TWO CIRCULATORY SYSTEMS

PULMONARY CIRCULATION

This system pumps blood from the heart to the lungs for oxygenation and back again. Blood is pumped from the heart out of the right ventricle into the pulmonary artery. This artery carries the blood, which contains low levels of oxygen and high levels of carbon dioxide, away from the heart. The pulmonary artery then splits into two with one branch going to the right lung and the other branch going to the left lung. The branches separate into **capillaries** in the lungs where **gaseous exchange** takes place (oxygen replaces carbon dioxide) in the alveoli. Oxygen attaches itself to **haemoglobin** in the red blood cells and then returns to the heart via pulmonary veins. In re-enters the heart through the left atrium and then fills the left ventricle ready to be pumped into the systemic circulation.

Pulmonary artery

Pulmonary capillary

Precava

Pulmonary vein

Right atrium

Postcava

Aorta

Right ventricle

Left atrium

Black blood

Left ventricle

Arterial blood

Capillaries of peripheral tissues

WOW!

The heart pumps around 60 to 100 times per minute but can go much faster if necessary to feed muscles with oxygen (their fuel). It beats around 100,000 a day, 30 million times a year and about 3 billion times in a lifetime.

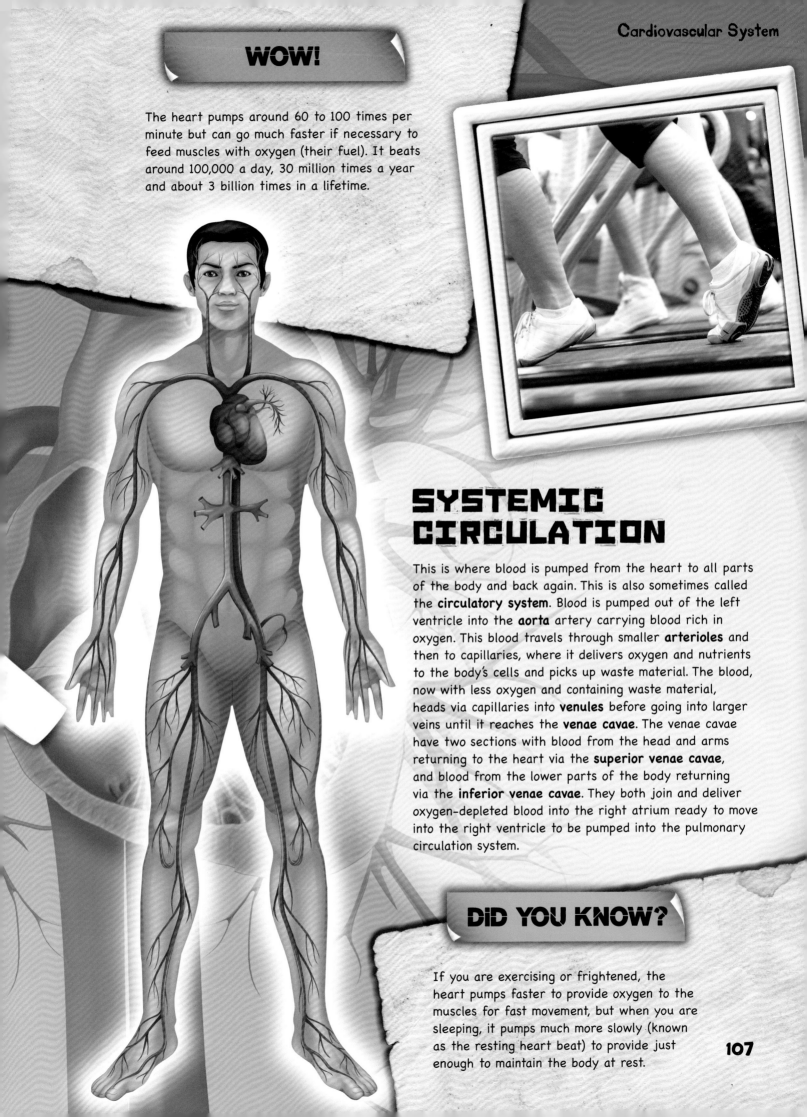

SYSTEMIC CIRCULATION

This is where blood is pumped from the heart to all parts of the body and back again. This is also sometimes called the **circulatory system**. Blood is pumped out of the left ventricle into the **aorta** artery carrying blood rich in oxygen. This blood travels through smaller **arterioles** and then to capillaries, where it delivers oxygen and nutrients to the body's cells and picks up waste material. The blood, now with less oxygen and containing waste material, heads via capillaries into **venules** before going into larger veins until it reaches the **venae cavae**. The venae cavae have two sections with blood from the head and arms returning to the heart via the **superior venae cavae**, and blood from the lower parts of the body returning via the **inferior venae cavae**. They both join and deliver oxygen-depleted blood into the right atrium ready to move into the right ventricle to be pumped into the pulmonary circulation system.

DID YOU KNOW?

If you are exercising or frightened, the heart pumps faster to provide oxygen to the muscles for fast movement, but when you are sleeping, it pumps much more slowly (known as the resting heart beat) to provide just enough to maintain the body at rest.

107

THE HEART

The heart is essential for your survival! Your heart is constantly working, even when you are resting.

The heart, blood and blood vessels together make up the circulatory system. The heart pumps the blood through the blood vessels to all the different tissues of the body. This blood carries water, oxygen and nutrients. Blood is also important for removing waste products from the body. The heart sits between the lungs in the chest, where it is well-protected by the rib cage.

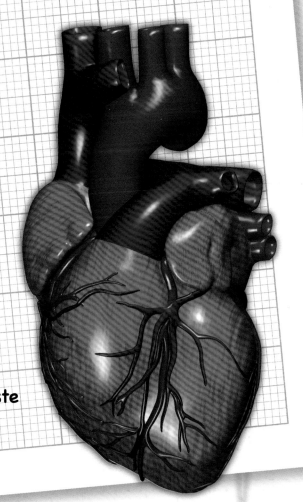

HOW COOL!

THE HEARTBEAT

The heart begins to beat just 3 weeks after conception, and continues to beat about 70 times a minute for your whole life!

The beating of the heart is what pushes the blood around the body. This is the action of two separate, but coordinated, pumps: the right side of the heart and the left side of the heart. Each pump has its own atrium, ventricle, inlet valve and outlet valve. Every heartbeat is initiated and controlled by electrical impulses. These can be measured using an electrocardiogram (ECG). These impulses cause the muscular chambers of the heart to contract, or squeeze, at different times. This squeezing action is what pushes the blood through the body.

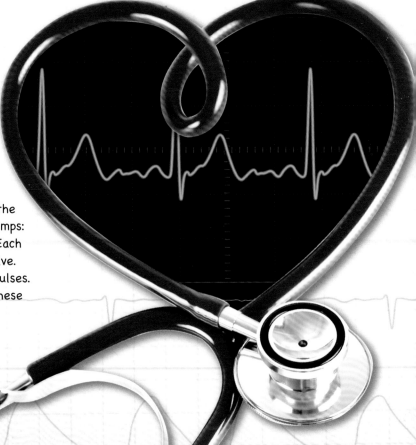

AMAZING!

BLOOD SUPPLY

Like any other muscle of the body, the heart needs a constant blood supply to stay healthy. It may seem as though the heart has easy access to lots of blood. However, the blood passing through the chambers of the heart does not actually supply oxygen and nutrients to the heart muscle.

Instead, special blood vessels, called coronary arteries, branch off from the aorta and deliver blood into the heart muscle itself. If there is a problem with the coronary arteries, the heart muscle will not get enough blood, and the heart will not be able to work properly.

SCAN ME
Instructions on page 5

SUPER FACT!

DID YOU KNOW?

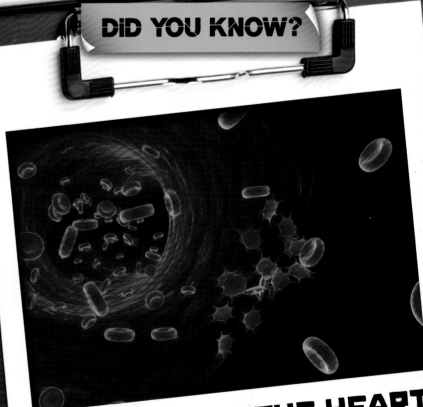

THE CONDUCTING SYSTEM

The heart contains a conducting system, which allows electrical currents to pass through it in a controlled way. These electrical currents control the heartbeat. The structures of the conducting system are made of special cells that initiate and conduct electricity. Cells that initiate an electrical impulse without any outside signal are called autorhythmic or pacemaker cells.

ANATOMY OF THE HEART

The heart is a hollow, muscular organ, composed of four chambers. Many different blood vessels enter and leave the heart. Blood vessels that carry blood away from the heart are called arteries; blood vessels that bring blood towards the heart are called veins.

109

THE HEART

Let's take a look at the heart in more detail with this cross-sectional illustration.

The heart has 4 main chambers:

Right atrium
This is found in the upper right-hand section of the heart. This is where oxygen-depleted (oxygen poor) blood arrives from the two major veins, the superior vena cava and the inferior vena cava. This blood is then pumped through the tricuspid valve into the right ventricle.

Right ventricle
The oxygen-depleted blood arrives from the right atrium, which is located just above the right ventricle. The blood is then pumped out via the pulmonary valve into the pulmonary artery to be taken to the lungs for re-oxygenation.

Left atrium
Located at the upper left-hand section of the heart, oxygen-rich blood arrives from the pulmonary veins. It is then pumped through the mitral valve into the left ventricle.

Left ventricle
The left ventricle is situated below the left atrium from where it receives oxygen-rich blood. This blood then gets pumped through the aortic valve into the aorta to be distributed throughout the entire body, including the heart itself via the coronary arteries.

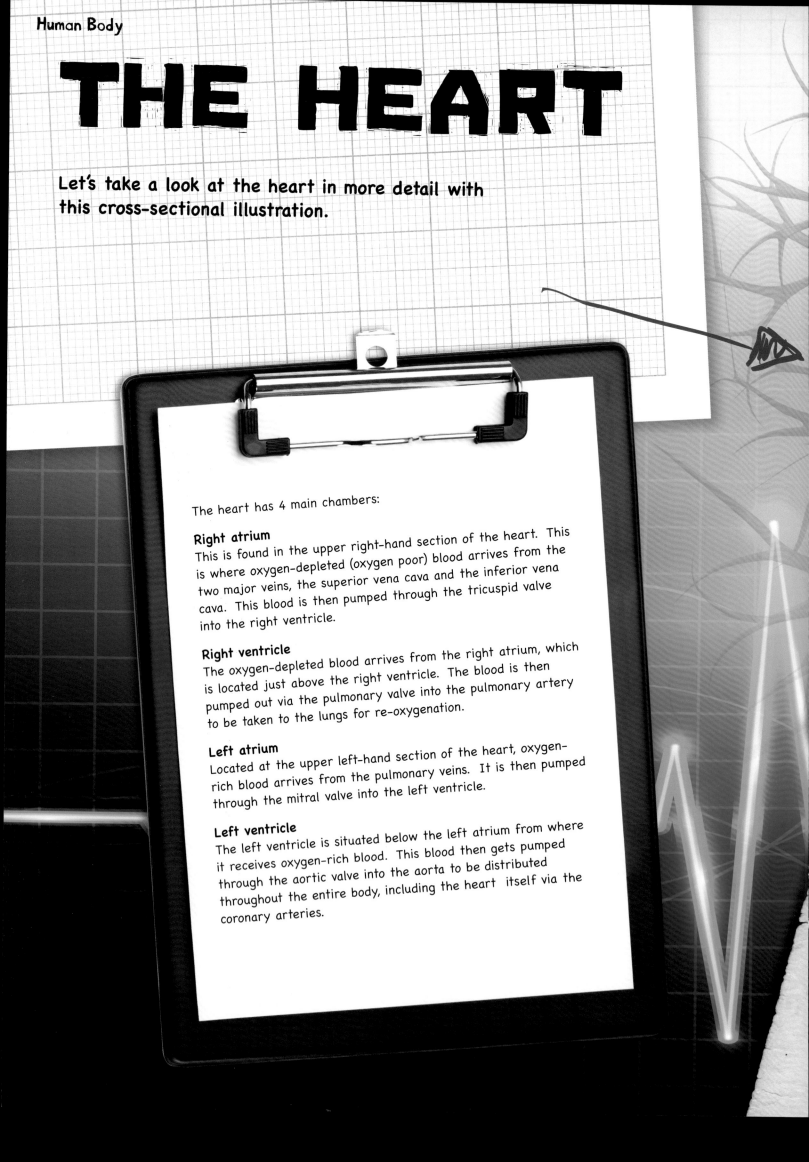

Internal anatomy of the heart

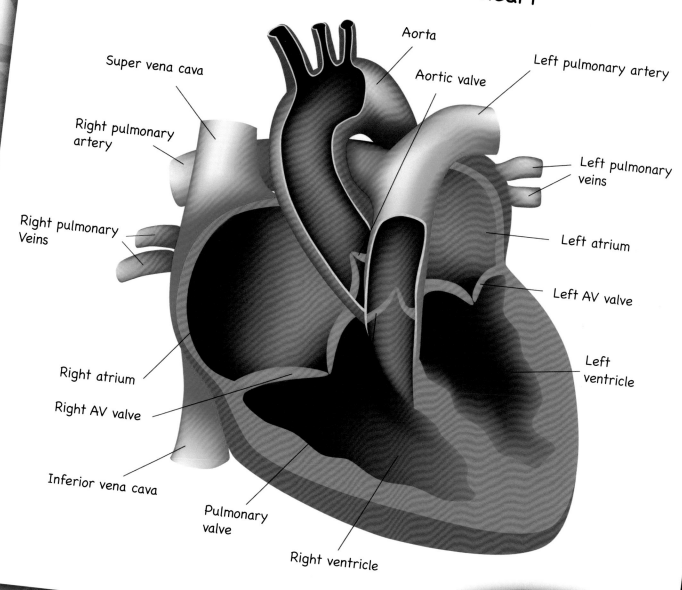

- Aorta
- Aortic valve
- Left pulmonary artery
- Super vena cava
- Right pulmonary artery
- Left pulmonary veins
- Right pulmonary Veins
- Left atrium
- Left AV valve
- Right atrium
- Right AV valve
- Left ventricle
- Inferior vena cava
- Pulmonary valve
- Right ventricle

DID YOU KNOW?

- Your heart is made up almost entirely of muscle. It is strong enough to lift approximately 3,000 pounds – roughly the weight of a compact car.

VALVES

Each of the heart's chambers has valves that are there to make sure blood flows in the right direction. These valves allow blood to pass through in one direction only so there can be no backflow of blood. There are four main valves in the heart.

Operatioin of the heart valves

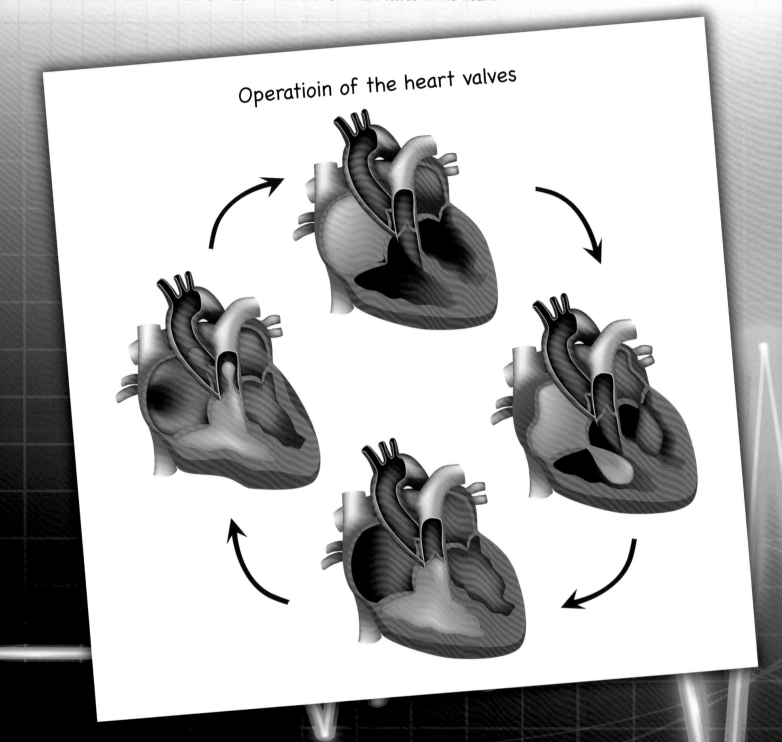

The Tricuspid Valve
The tricuspid valve is found between the right atrium and the right ventricle and allows oxygen-depleted blood to flow from the right atrium into the right ventricle.

The Pulmonary Valve
The pulmonary valve is located between the right ventricle and the pulmonary artery. It allows the flow of oxygen-depleted blood to be pumped out of the heart into the pulmonary artery to go to the lungs for re-oxygenation.

The Mitral Valve
Located between the left atrium and the left ventricle, the mitral valve permits oxygenated blood to be pumped into the left ventricle.

The Aortic Valve
The aortic valve is located between the left ventricle and the aorta allowing blood to be pumped out from the heart into the aorta for distribution around the body.

HEARTY FACTS

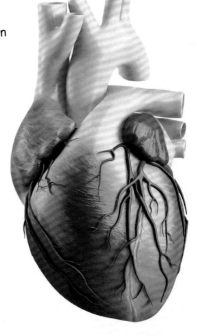

- The heart is fully developed after 8 weeks from conception, this is when an embryo is only an inch long.

- The heart weighs less than one pound. The average weight for women is eight ounces and for men, 10 ounces.

- Your heartbeats with enough strength to shoot blood a distance of 30 feet.

- Your left lung is smaller than your right one to make room in your chest cavity for your heart.

- On average, a million barrels' worth of blood is pumped through the heart in a lifetime.

- Clench your fists and put them side by side. This is roughly the size of your heart.

- Women's hearts beat faster than men's hearts.

120/60
23:20

BLOOD

Blood is the red stuff that oozes out when you get a cut. It is very important as it is the fluid that travels throughout your body from your head to your toes and keeps your body going. Like a transport system, it carries oxygen and nourishment from digested food to every part of the body and removes the waste we don't need. Blood helps us fight infections and keeps the body healthy. It also acts as a temperature regulator, stopping us getting too hot or too cold. The average adult has about 10 pints (5.7 litres) of blood in their bodies.

WHAT'S IN OUR BLOOD?

Our blood has three main ingredients:

Red blood cells – these give our blood its red color, and they carry oxygen from the lungs throughout the body. They are the most common cells in our body.

White blood cells – are like the body's soldiers, they help guard the body against invasion from germs.

Platelets – are the cells that clot the blood and stop you bleeding if you get a cut.

These ingredients are carried in **plasma**, a yellowish liquid which makes up half of the blood in your body. Its job is to carry the nutrients, hormones and proteins to all the parts of the body. Plasma is mainly made up of water.

HOW COOL!

Half of your body's red blood cells are replaced every seven days.

One drop of blood contains 5 million red blood cells, 7,000 white blood cells, 500,000 platelet cells, together with water, sugar, salt, hormones, vitamins, fat and protein!

HOW DOES BLOOD TRAVEL ROUND OUR BODIES?

Blood travels round the body in a highly effective system called the **circulation system**. Pumped by the heart, our blood is carried around in tubes called arteries and veins, which are known as the body's blood vessels.

Arteries - carry blood and oxygen from your heart to the rest of your body.

Veins - transport the blood back to the heart.

Capillaries - these are tiny blood vessels that carry blood between the smallest arteries and smallest veins.

AWESOME!

There are around 60,000 miles of blood vessels in your body!

It takes less than 60 seconds to pump blood to every cell in your body.

BLOOD TRANSFUSIONS

Sometimes people need more blood than their bodies can produce, for example if you lose blood during an accident. In these cases, you need a blood transfusion, which replaces the blood you have lost. This is normally done in hospital and takes between 1 to 4 hours depending on how much blood is needed. Hospitals store blood in a blood bank and it is collected from volunteer donors. The blood is stored in separate supplies of cells and plasma.

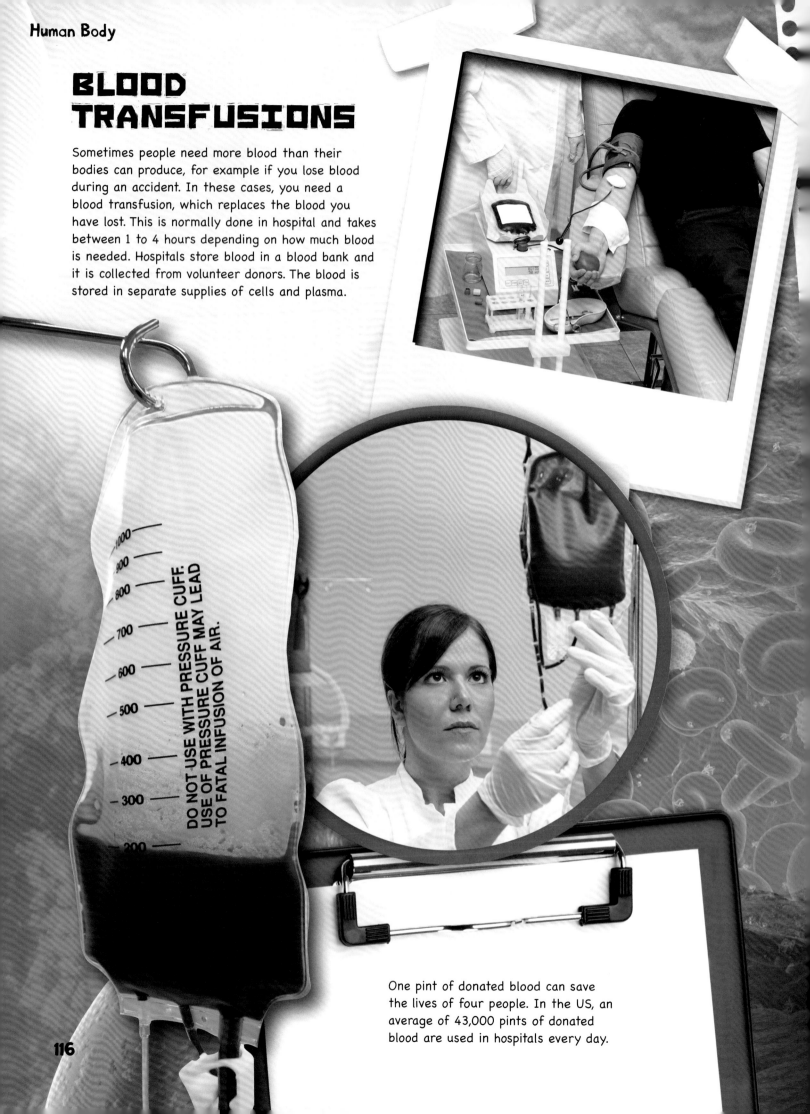

DO NOT USE WITH PRESSURE CUFF.
USE OF PRESSURE CUFF MAY LEAD
TO FATAL INFUSION OF AIR.

One pint of donated blood can save the lives of four people. In the US, an average of 43,000 pints of donated blood are used in hospitals every day.

Your blood gets thicker the higher you climb up a mountain. This is because the blood needs to make extra red blood cells to carry more oxygen round the body as the air has less oxygen in high altitude areas.

BLOOD TYPES

There are four different types of blood and these are called blood groups. Blood groups are important because our bodies will only accept blood that is compatible with our own blood group, and will attack and destroy cells in another blood group it doesn't recognise.

Blood group A - can only give blood to people with A or AB blood groups.

Blood group AB - can only give blood to people with AB.

Blood group O - O can donate blood to anyone.

Blood group B - can only give blood to people with B or AB.

DID YOU KNOW?

The heart pumps over 300 million liters of blood around the body in an average life time. That's enough blood to fill 5,500 large swimming pools!

ARTERIES AND VEINS

Arteries and veins are the fuel lines and plumbing in your body. These blood vessels (arteries and veins) carry blood all over your body and deliver the oxygen, nutrients from food and hormones required as well as clearing all the waste products such as carbon dioxide.

circulatory system

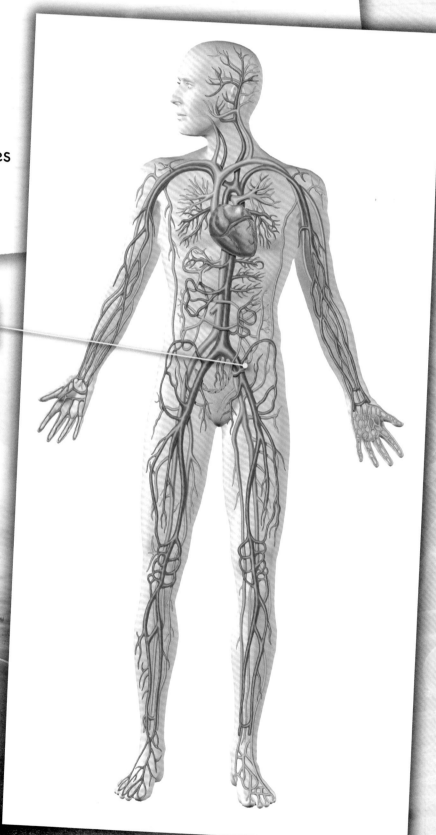

YOU'RE KIDDING?

If all the blood vessels in your body were laid end to end, they would reach about 60,000 miles.

ARTERIES

Arteries are the thickest blood vessels and have muscular walls that contract helping the blood carry on through the body. There are two major arteries and both start at the heart — one is called the **aorta** and the other the **pulmonary artery**. The aorta has oxygen-rich blood pumped into it from the heart at the start of a circulatory process called **systemic circulation**. The aorta goes through the center of your body and branches off into other arteries in the direction of the head and neck, and arms and legs. From
these main arteries there are more branching out into **arterioles**, which are smaller and less elastic. The arterioles then spread out into a network of tiny **capillaries**. It is through the capillaries that the nutrients and oxygen are delivered to the cells. The capillaries also connect to the veins so that as the blood from the arteries delivers the oxygen to the cells it picks up waste, namely carbon dioxide, and returns via the capillaries to the veins.

It is a myth that arteries only carry oxygen-rich blood. The other major artery connected to the heart is the pulmonary artery. The heart pumps de-oxygenated blood (oxygen poor) into the pulmonary artery from a different chamber than the aorta. The pulmonary artery heads to the lungs, splitting into two. One branch goes to the left lung and the other branch goes to the right lung. The artery further branches out into arterioles which in turn spread out across the lungs into tiny capillaries ready to pick up oxygen and return via capillaries and veins to the heart for pumping around the body.

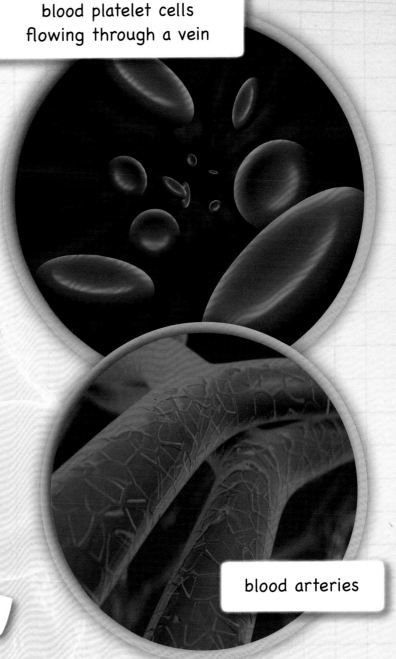

blood platelet cells
flowing through a vein

blood arteries

FAT FACT!

Every pound of fat gained causes your body to make 7 new miles of blood vessels. This extra distance means your heart has to work much harder to pump blood around the body which is why being overweight is so unhealthy.

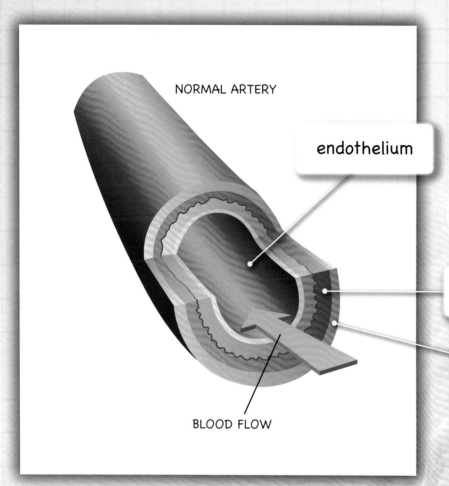

NORMAL ARTERY

endothelium

media

adventitia

BLOOD FLOW

STRONG PIPES

The wall of the arteries have three layers:

1. The **endothelium** is on the inside and has a smooth lining for blood to flow over.

2. The **media** is the middle part of the artery and is a layer of muscle and elastic tissue.

3. The **adventitia** is a tough covering that protects the outside of the artery.

VEINS

Veins are made up of the same material as arteries but they are not as muscular or as thick. They carry blood back to the heart. As they are not as muscular to stop blood flowing back on itself, veins have valves allowing blood to flow only one way. There are two major veins called the superior vena cava and the inferior vena cava, one above the heart and the other below. In the pulmonary circulatory system, the vein takes oxygen rich blood from the lungs to the heart ready to be pumped around the body. In the systemic circulatory system, the veins take deoxygenated blood from the capillaries back to the heart to be pumped towards the lungs.

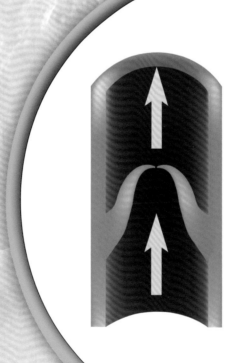

CHOC-TASTIC

Some scientists have suggested that chocolate can improve your cardiovascular health. Cocoa, the main ingredient in chocolate, contains antioxidants that can help lower blood pressure meaning your heart does not have to work so hard.

MYTH BUSTER

Despite popular belief, veins are not blue in color and neither is the blood blue. Many people believe the blue color of veins, when seen through the skin, is due to the blood being deoxygenized and so the blood is also blue in color. In fact, veins appear blue through the skin as a result of light penetrating the skin and changing the color of what we actually see.

NOSE

Our noses are very important pieces of human equipment. We use them to smell and taste but also to protect our bodies from infections.

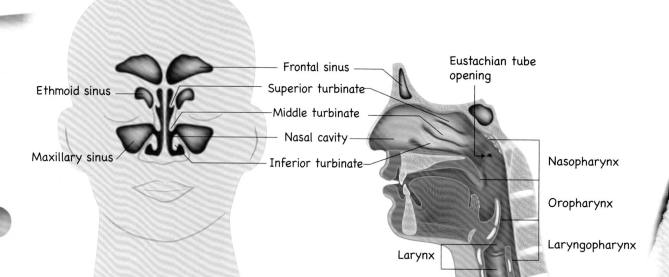

Ethmoid sinus

Frontal sinus

Superior turbinate

Middle turbinate

Nasal cavity

Maxillary sinus

Inferior turbinate

Eustachian tube opening

Nasopharynx

Oropharynx

Laryngopharynx

Larynx

SMELLS GOOD

Did you know most of our taste is actually smell? The back of your mouth is linked to your nose so you can smell food as you chew it.

EWW, BOOGERS

When we get a cold, tiny hairs in our nose get clogged with gunky mucus. This can stop us from smelling and even tasting. The mucus is created as a side effect of our nose trying to beat the infection.

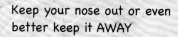
Keep your nose out or even better keep it AWAY

122

DiD YOU KNOW?

Did you know that the air from a sneeze can travel at speeds of 100 miles per hour or more? This is another good reason to cover your nose and mouth when you sneeze, or to duck when you hear one coming your way.

AMAZING!

FAMOUS SNOZZLES

ALBERT WEBER - American organoleptic analyst

His nose was his livelihood as he was an official smeller. He was the dean of two dozen organoleptic analysts (food sniffers) working for the U.S. Food and Drug Administration. According to a well-known source "Webber was a graduate chemist and was testing food with his test tubes and microscopes in the FDA's New York District Laboratory in Manhattan in 1943, when a call came in from the Boston office. A shipment of suspect ocean perch was on its way. There was no way to test chemically for partly decomposed fish - they have to be smelled. Weber was elected that day and worked as a sniffer for over 35 years, sniffing everything from dog food to soft drinks...."

SNNOSE JOKE

Although we do not have a nose as sensitive as a dog's, we can still remember over 50,000 smells.

PINOCCHIO

We all know the story of Pinocchio and his long wooden nose. Every time Pinocchio lied his nose would grow longer! So make sure you always tell the truth!

RESPIRATORY SYSTEM AND THE LUNGS

The respiratory system enables the body to breathe in oxygen from the air around us and breathe out carbon dioxide. The body has billions of cells that need a constant supply of oxygen to enable them to release energy from the food you have eaten. This energy keeps all the cells that make up your body alive. The waste from the cells' energy is released as carbon dioxide, which is poisonous to the cells and is removed from the body when we breathe out.

The main organ in the respiratory system is the lungs. We have two lungs, one on each side of the chest, separated by the heart and protected by the bony rib cage.

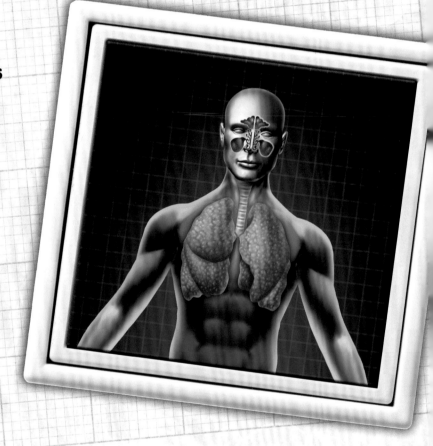

HOW COOL!

The movement of air into the lungs starts by breathing air in through the nose or mouth and into the windpipe (also called the trachea). The air then goes through the bronchus into the bronchioles and finally into the alveoli, which are little air sacs in the lungs. The oxygen in the air in the alveoli is exchanged into the blood and the carbon dioxide from the blood exchanged into the air sacs to be breathed out. The oxygen now in the blood is taken by the pulmonary vein to the heart where it can be pumped all around the body and supply oxygen to all the cells.

AWESOME FACT

As you breathe in, your lungs stretch out to take in lots of air but as you breathe out, your lungs then squash down and force out all of the air. Breathing is helped by the ribs and the diaphragm, which is a muscle sitting underneath the lungs. When your lungs fill with air, your rib cage rises outwards and then lowers as the air goes out. This is helped by the diaphragm moving down and up as you breathe in and out.

Inspiration

Expiration

DID YOU KNOW?

Your lungs are just like a rabbit warren, with lots of tunnels ending in tiny air sacs which are called alveoli. But it is not rabbits running around these tunnels but oxygen from the air you breathe. The oxygen enters all of these tunnels as you breathe in and races around until it reaches all the alveoli. The alveoli are covered in tiny blood capillaries, which take the oxygen into the blood and carry it around your whole body.

Let's take a look at the lungs in more detail with this cross-section picture.

From the outside, lungs look like a pair of spongy bags that sit inside your ribs, but the inside is filled with 'high-tech' breathing technology that keeps you alive. Two large tubes called the bronchi connect the lungs to the bottom of the trachea and these then branch off into tubes (or bronchi) that get smaller and smaller, finally connecting to the 30,000 tiny bronchioles (tubes). An easy way to imagine the bronchi is picturing them like a big tree.

The Respiratory System

Nasal cavity
Nostril
Epiglottis
Larynx
Pharynx
Trachea
Pleural cavity
Primary bronchus
Right lung
Diaphragm
Left lung

At the end of each bronchiole are special little air sacs called alveoli. There are about 600 million alveoli in your lungs and if you stretched them out, they would cover an entire tennis court. The oxygen from the air we breathe ends up in the alveoli. Each alveoli has a mesh-like covering of very small blood vessels called capillaries. These capillaries exchange oxygen into the blood from the air you have breathed in and carbon dioxide from the blood is in turn exchanged through the alveoli to be breathed out. The oxygen, which has now been transferred into the blood, is taken by the pulmonary vein to the heart where it can be pumped all around the body and supply oxygen to cells.

This process of breathing in and out is an automatic action triggered by the level of carbon dioxide in the blood and this is controlled by the **medulla oblongata** in the base of the brain.

The **diaphragm** is a thin, dome-shaped muscle below your lungs which helps you breathe and separates the lungs from your stomach and intestines. When you breathe in, your diaphragm tightens and moves downward. This increases the space in your chest cavity so that your lungs can expand.

KEEPING YOUR LUNGS HEALTHY

Smoking isn't good for any part of your body, and your lungs especially hate it. Cigarette smoke damages the cilia in the trachea, stopping them from keeping dirt and other substances out of the lungs. The chemicals in cigarette smoke damage the alveoli and can cause the walls of the alveoli to break down, making it much harder to breathe. Cigarette smoke can also damage the cells of the lungs, destroying the healthy cells and replacing them with cancer cells.

If you need to work with chemicals in an art or chemistry class, make sure you wear a protective mask to keep chemical fumes from entering your lungs.

FUN FACT!

The alveoli in the lungs look like tiny bunches of grapes. A diet high in fresh grapes has been shown to reduce the risk of lung cancer and emphysema (lung disease).

LUNG FACTS

- Alveoli do not begin to form until week 23 to 24 of pregnancy, which is one reason why very premature babies struggle to survive.

- You can live with one lung. It limits your physical ability but doesn't stop you from living a relatively normal life. Many people around the world live with just one lung.

- People who have a large lung capacity can send oxygen around their body faster. You can increase your lung capacity with regular exercise.

- When resting, the average adult breathes around 12 to 20 times a minute.

- An average person breathes in around 11,000 litres of air every day.

THE DIGESTIVE SYSTEM

The digestive system is made up of a lot of hollow organs contained within a long twisted tube, just like a sausage without any filling. This is called the digestive tract.

The digestive tract starts at the mouth and goes all the way through the torso to the anus. Organs that make up the digestive tract are the mouth, esophagus, stomach, small intestine, large intestine, rectum, and anus.

WHY AM I IMPORTANT?

The main role of the digestive system is to help the body grow and to provide energy, which in turn gives humans the ability to live.

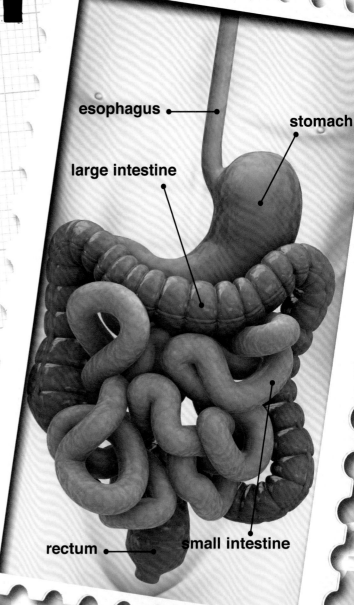

esophagus

stomach

large intestine

small intestine

rectum

DON'T FORGET US

Two other organs that make up the digestive system are the pancreas and liver, both of which play a crucial role within the human body.

EWW, GROSS!

If you happen to get germs or a virus in your stomach, or you eat food with a lot of **bacteria** in it, or you feel nervous, or subject your body to movement (such as a car journey), then sometimes the stomach or intestines try to keep hold of the food by applying muscles to push food back up rather than down. This carries on until it reaches the mouth, making you vomit.

THE DIGESTIVE JOURNEY

Food is put in the mouth and **saliva** helps soften it as it is chewed by the mouth into small pieces, before it goes down a long tube, called the **esophagus**.

Food is then held in the **stomach**, where it is processed by the stomach muscles and enzymes and is turned into a liquid called **chyme** which slowly drips into the **small intestine**.

The stomach and small intestine take virtually all of the **nutrients** out of the chyme leaving just water, bacteria, fiber, dead cells and anything else that the body cannot absorb.

This waste and water then pass into the **large intestine** (which contains the liver, pancreas and gallbladder) where all of the remaining water is absorbed and the leftover waste matter is compressed into **feces**, before leaving the body, out of the anus and into our toilets as poop.

129

STOMACH

You start to digest your food from the moment it enters your mouth. Enzymes in your saliva (spit) start to break down the food. Enzymes are natural substances (proteins) that speed up chemical reactions (catalysts).

As your saliva moistens the passage down the throat, food passes down there easily after being torn apart by your front teeth and chewed and mashed up by your back teeth. Your strong, muscly tongue also helps send food down to your stomach.

SCAN ME
Instructions on page 5

ACID BATH

The stomach is J-shaped and is on the upper left side of the abdomen. An adult stomach is about 10 inches (25 cm) long but can easily expand to hold about a quart (a liter) of food.

When the food reaches the stomach it gets soaked in very strong acid that breaks down all of the different molecules in the food. The stomach walls are made of four layers and the innermost layer has glands that secrete (release) acid and enzymes to do all the hard work.

WOULDN'T ACID BURN A WHOLE THROUGH YOU?

It certainly would, but you get a new stomach lining every three to four days. If you didn't, the strong acids your stomach uses to digest food would also digest your stomach.

DIGESTING A MEAL

Once food is chewed and swallowed there is a long journey of digestion that can take over a day. There are many different organs and enzymes that work at digesting different parts of the meal. Starch (bread, pasta) for example starts to get broken down by the saliva in the mouth. Proteins have to wait until the strong acid in the stomach.

DID YOU KNOW?

The word stomach is derived from the Greek word stomachos. The Greek word stomachos is derived from stoma meaning mouth.

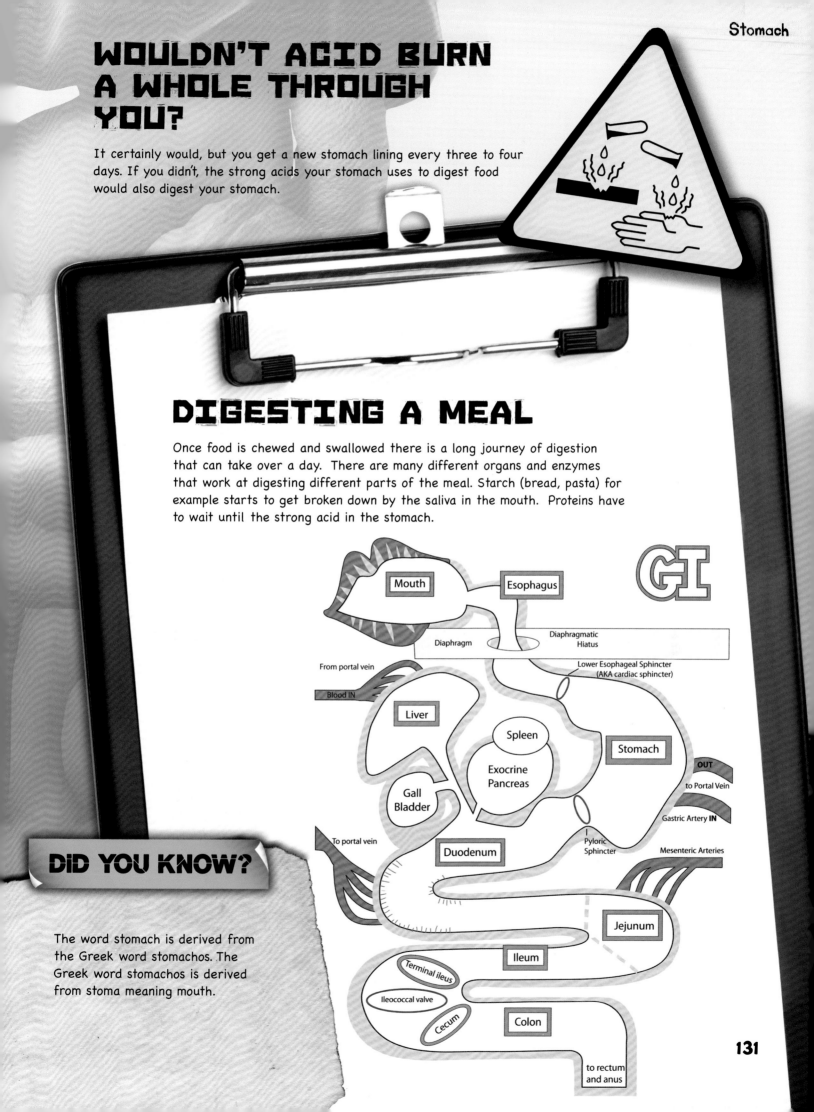

GI

Mouth

Esophagus

Diaphragm

Diaphragmatic Hiatus

From portal vein

Lower Esophageal Sphincter
(AKA cardiac sphincter)

Blood IN

Liver

Spleen

Stomach

Exocrine Pancreas

OUT
to Portal Vein

Gall Bladder

Gastric Artery IN

To portal vein

Pyloric Sphincter

Mesenteric Arteries

Duodenum

Jejunum

Ileum

Terminal ileus

Ileococcal valve

Cecum

Colon

to rectum and anus

FOOD SWALLOWED AT LUNCH

After a bit of chewing it takes around 10-15 seconds for swallowed food to arrive in the stomach.

STOMACH TIME

Food usually spends around four hours being broken down in the stomach. Although if it is rich food this can take longer.

HOW COOL!

People can, and have, lived without a stomach if it has been removed because of illness!

Inside the stomach there is hydrochloric acid which kills bacteria and provides acidic conditions for the enzyme protease.

When you blush, the lining of your stomach also turns red.

When we swallow our food, we also swallow air. This air causes most of the gas in your stomach and intestinal tract.

The best way to get rid of this air is to burp!

GREMLINS IN MY INTESTINES

As the food leaves the stomach it gets pushed slowly through the small intestine and can sometimes cause loud grumbling, bubbly noises.

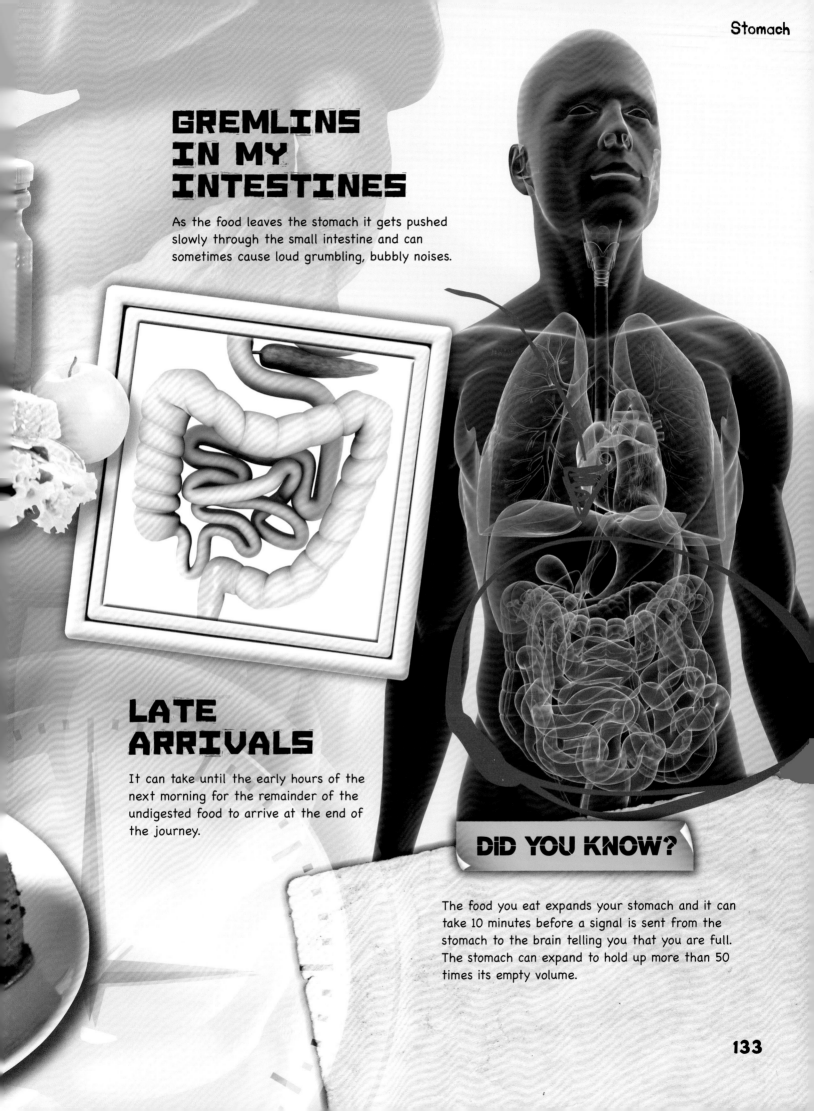

LATE ARRIVALS

It can take until the early hours of the next morning for the remainder of the undigested food to arrive at the end of the journey.

DID YOU KNOW?

The food you eat expands your stomach and it can take 10 minutes before a signal is sent from the stomach to the brain telling you that you are full. The stomach can expand to hold up more than 50 times its empty volume.

133

INTESTINES

The intestine, also known as your guts, is a long tube that starts at the bottom of the stomach and finishes at the anus. It plays an essential role in your digestive system and processes all of the food you eat and passes all the non-digestible food through your body to come out as waste, also known as feces or POOP!

The intestine is actually split into two parts with two functions. There is the **small intestine** and the **large intestine**. The small intestine is the thinner tube that starts at the stomach and winds around until it becomes wider. This is where it turns into the large intestine.

STRING OF SAUSAGES

The small intestine is around 6 meters long, 2.5cm wide and is the longest part of the digestive system. Even though it is longer than the larger intestine, it is called the small intestine because it is thinner. There are three parts to the small intestine, called the **duodenum**, **jejunum** and **ileum**. The stomach churns up the food that you have eaten and squirts small amounts into the top part of the small intestine, the duodenum. It is here that bile from the gall bladder and digestive juices from the pancreas break down the rest of the food. This releases nutrients which are absorbed by the intestinal walls and start to enter the bloodstream as the food and waste move through the small intestine. The waste then moves into the large intestine for further processing.

MUSCULAR MOTION

Digesting food is moved through the small intestine by waves of muscle contraction and relaxation. This process is called peristalsis and it squeezes food along the digestive tract.

VILE VILLI

Nutrients are absorbed all along the walls of the small intestine. To help with the absorption and make it quicker, the walls are lined with microscopic finger-like protrusions called villi and microvilli. These increase the surface area and also give the inside of your intestine the look and feel of velvet.

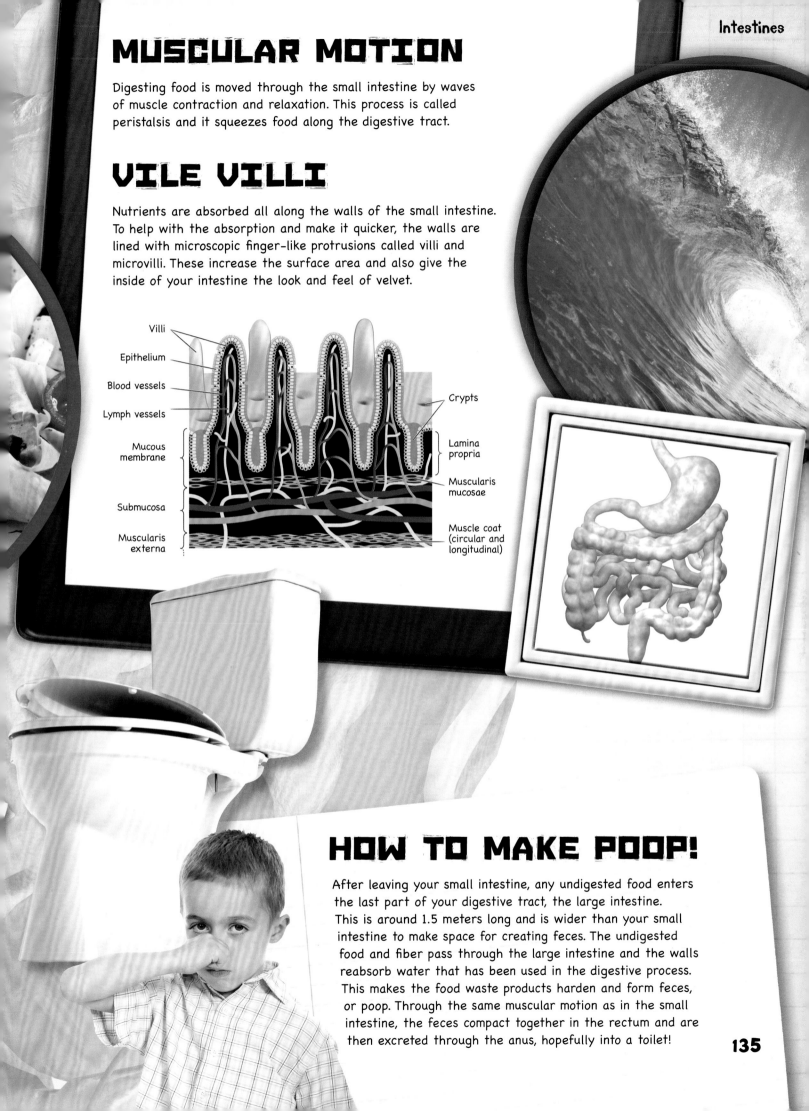

Villi
Epithelium
Blood vessels
Lymph vessels
Mucous membrane
Submucosa
Muscularis externa
Crypts
Lamina propria
Muscularis mucosae
Muscle coat (circular and longitudinal)

HOW TO MAKE POOP!

After leaving your small intestine, any undigested food enters the last part of your digestive tract, the large intestine. This is around 1.5 meters long and is wider than your small intestine to make space for creating feces. The undigested food and fiber pass through the large intestine and the walls reabsorb water that has been used in the digestive process. This makes the food waste products harden and form feces, or poop. Through the same muscular motion as in the small intestine, the feces compact together in the rectum and are then excreted through the anus, hopefully into a toilet!

KIDNEYS

The kidneys are organs that clean and filter your blood. We normally have two kidneys and you need at least one to stay alive. The kidneys are found at the bottom of the rib cage at the back of the body and there is one on each side of your spine. Kidneys are bean-shaped and about 13 centimeters long. They are each about the size of a computer mouse or a fist.

HOW DO THEY WORK?

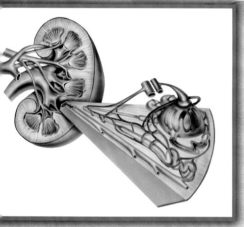

Blood flows into the kidneys through the renal arteries and then passes through a series of blood vessels that get smaller and smaller leading to tiny filtering units called **nephrons**, into which blood is forced at high pressure. The nephrons clean the blood, and produce urine (pee) from waste products the body doesn't need. The urine is sent down a tube called the ureter and collects in the bladder, which is a storage device for holding urine. Once the bladder is half full, it signals to the brain that you need to go to the bathroom and the urine is expelled from the body down another tube called the **urethra** when we pee. The clean blood is reabsorbed into the body.

The kidneys also control the water levels in your body. If you drink too much, your kidneys get rid of the excess water by producing watery pale urine. If your body is short of water the kidneys don't pass as much through into your urine, you pee less and your urine will be much darker.

The brain and kidneys communicate through hormones which tell the kidneys whether to keep or expel fluids. If you feel thirsty, your brain is telling you to drink more fluids to keep your body as balanced as possible.

A BALANCING ACT!

Another job of the kidneys is to balance the volume of fluids and minerals in the body. This is called **homeostasis**.

The amount of water we take into our bodies and the amount of water our bodies get rid of needs to balance, like these scales.

Our bodies get water when we drink water or other liquids. We also get water from some foods, like fruits and vegetables.

Water leaves our bodies in several ways. Urine makes up more than half the water we expel in pee. Breath contains around a quarter of the water our bodies get rid of. Sweat counts for a 12th of the water we dispose off and finally a small amount comes out in poop!

DID YOU KNOW?

Your blood pressure is controlled by the amount of water in your blood.

AWESOME!

The blood flow through the kidneys is higher than even the brain, liver or heart. Did you also know that kidneys also produce a hormone that tells the body to make red blood cells?

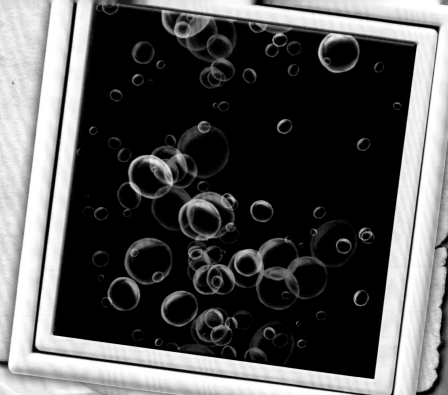

WOW FACT

25 min

Your kidneys filter your blood around 400 times a day. It takes around 25 minutes to clean all the blood in the body.

DID YOU KNOW?

Kidney stones are caused by clumps of crystals forming in the kidneys. Most kidney stones are very small and can be passed out in the urine. The largest kidney stone ever found was the size of a small coconut. That one had to be removed by surgery!

FUN FACT

Our kidneys look just like kidney beans. Kidney beans are actually very good for the kidneys and help heal and maintain kidney function. Kidney beans provide a variety of minerals and vitamins and so are generally good for your health.

WHAT A LOT OF PEE!

A grown-up can produce one or two liters of pee every day. That would work out as 40,000 liters during an average lifespan!

THE NERVOUS SYSTEM

The world wide web (or the internet) is a global system of networked computers all communicating with each other in the same language and providing information to billions of users all over the world. If the internet suddenly didn't exist, or one part of it was very badly damaged, then until it could be repaired our modern global society would suffer and in some cases be paralyzed. The internet is used to communicate in so many different parts of our lives. The nervous system within our body is exactly the same. It acts as the communication network, taking electrical messages to and from the brain all around the body.

WOW AMAZING

The brain contains nerve cells which look like alien starfish and these cells send and receive electrical messages through the nerve network around the body. Information is sent to the brain from the five senses (sight, hearing, taste, smell and touch) and the brain decides what to do and then sends the response. This information travels very fast and is like lots of small flashes of lightning.

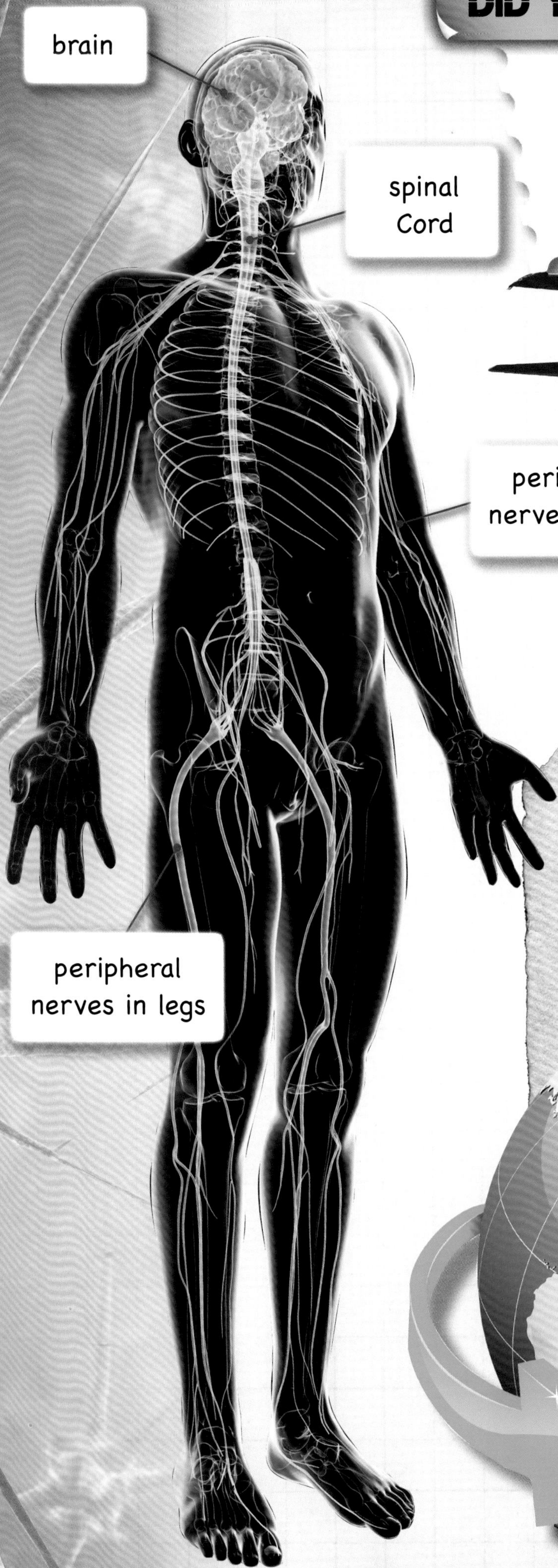

brain

spinal Cord

peripheral nerves in arm

peripheral nerves in legs

DID YOU KNOW?

The electrical messages that are sent around the nervous system travel at about 270mph. A modern jet taking off achieves at take off only about 200mph.

AMAZING FACT

If you took all of the nerves that are inside the human body and laid them out in one long line, it would be about 30,000 miles long. To show you how awesome that is, if you started on one side of the earth and walked around the globe until you got back to where you started, you would still have enough to go further. Or think about this Japanese cyclist: in 2001 he started to ride through 37 countries. He finished in 2009, taking eight years to complete his journey and totalling around 30,000 miles on his bicycle.

THE BRAIN

The brain looks like a mass of gray jelly and is very soft. It is protected in a hard, bony case, called the skull. The human brain is quite large, but is wrinkled, which makes it compact.

The brain is the body's control center. It is involved with what we do and what we think as well as what we feel and remember. We also use our brain to learn. The left side of our brain controls the right side of our body and the right side of our brain controls the left side of our body.

Most people are right-handed because the left side of the brain is generally used more than the right side. Each side of our brain is responsible for different skills; the right side holds our artistic talent and imagination, while the left side is more responsible for practical abilities and logical thinking.

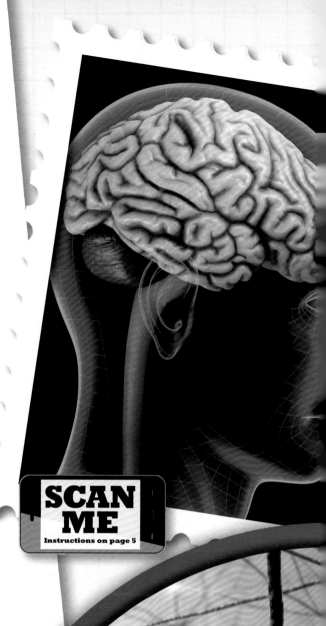

SCAN ME
Instructions on page 5

BRAIN SECTIONS

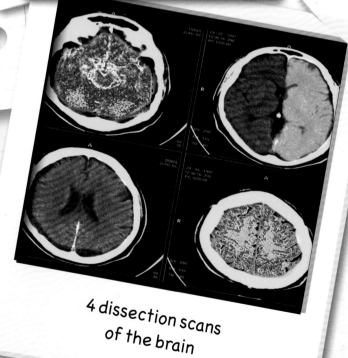

4 dissection scans of the brain

AWESOME FACT!

LEFT SIDE

- Scientific skills
- Writing
- Speech
- Logical and mathematical skills

RIGHT SIDE

- 3-dimensional awareness
- Artistic ability
- Musical ability
- Left-handed control

BRAIN CELLS

The cells that make up the brain are called neurons. Branches from the cells, called dendrites, receive impulses from the nerves while axons transmit them. Our brain interprets the impulses and can tell where they are coming from and what they are referring to. The brain cells can also store information. A piece of stored information is called memory. One part of our brain stores long-term memories, another part more recent memories.

DID YOU KNOW?

THE CEREBRUM

The largest part of the brain consists of two sections. Together they are known as the cerebral hemisphere, or cerebrum. The cerebrum is highly organized. It is arranged in different areas that relate to different parts of the body and to different needs. Vision is interpreted at the back of the cerebrum, hearing and speech at the side. The areas for sensation and movement are in the middle. The area at the front of the cerebrum, the frontal lobes, controls our behaviour. Below and to the back of the cerebrum lies the cerebellum. This contains nerve cells that are mainly concerned with balance. Below this, the brain is connected to the rest of the body by the spinal cord.

143

Our brain is at the center of our nervous system and acts like a powerful computer that stores our memories and controls how we think and act. Evolution has made our brains incredibly complicated, with many interesting properties that scientists still do not fully understand today. This is perhaps why 'to be a brain surgeon' is used as an expression to talk about someone who is fantastically clever, because you need to be clever to understand the brain. The **cranium** (human skull), which is made up of 22 bones that fuse together, protects the brain. It works together with **cerebrospinal fluid**, which is a liquid that the brain floats in. This fluid provides a cushion against physical impact and helps prevent infections. There are billions of nerve cells in the brain that send and receive information.

NEURONS

Neurons (nerve cells) are found in every part of the brain and throughout the nervous system. There are over 100 billion neurons in your body and they are truly amazing cells. Each neuron communicates with between 1,000 and 10,000 other cells through a section called a **dendrite** that gathers information and an **axon** that transmits information to other cells.

There are gaps called **synapses** between the neurons, so in order to communicate they have to release chemical molecules called **neurotransmitters.** These neurotransmitters carry nerve impulses across the synapses to the other cells.

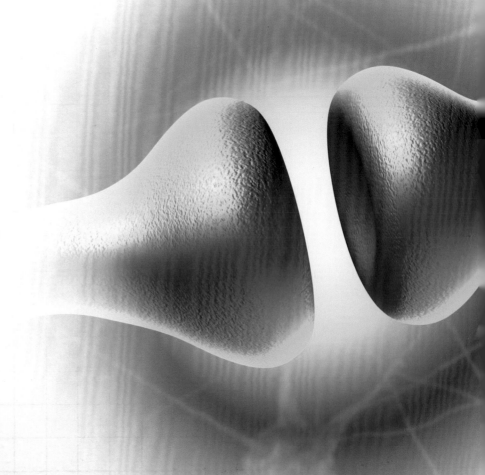

The communication across these gaps travels incredibly quickly. Just think that when you touch something, the neurons 'fire' from your hand all the way up to your brain where the impulses are deciphered and then you understand or know if what you are feeling, for example, is it soft, hard, liquid or solid. If you are touching something that you have never touched before, for example, shark skin, your brain can 'save' that information about how it feels by transferring impulses to the memory.

Your nervous system, particularly the brain, plays an incredibly important part in making us human and in how we make sense of the world around us. Sometimes this system malfunctions, such as in people with mental disorders, which can have dramatic effects on how they behave and what they understand.

BRAIN BOX MYTHS

- You only use 10 per cent of your brain. This is not true, even though this myth is considered common knowledge. No one is sure where this myth began. In fact, you use your entire brain.

- A person's personality displays right-brain or left-brain dominance. This myth suggests that a right-brain person is more creative and arty while a left-brain person is more logical and a problem-solver. It came about as a result of scientific investigation in the 1800s. Patients with injuries to the left or right side of the brain lost specific abilities. However, modern investigation using brain scanning technology proves that the left and right sides of the brain are very much dependent on each other. Having said that, the right-hand side of the brain does control the left-hand side of your body and vice versa.

- Brain damage is always permanent. This is not true because the brain can actually repair itself or compensate for certain losses. The brain even has the ability to create new cells. This ability was only recently discovered and proven in 1998.

145

STROKES

A stroke can cause loss of memory and physical function. Most strokes come about from a blood clot in the brain that blocks the local blood supply. This causes the damage or destruction of nearby brain tissue and produces a wide range of stroke symptoms.

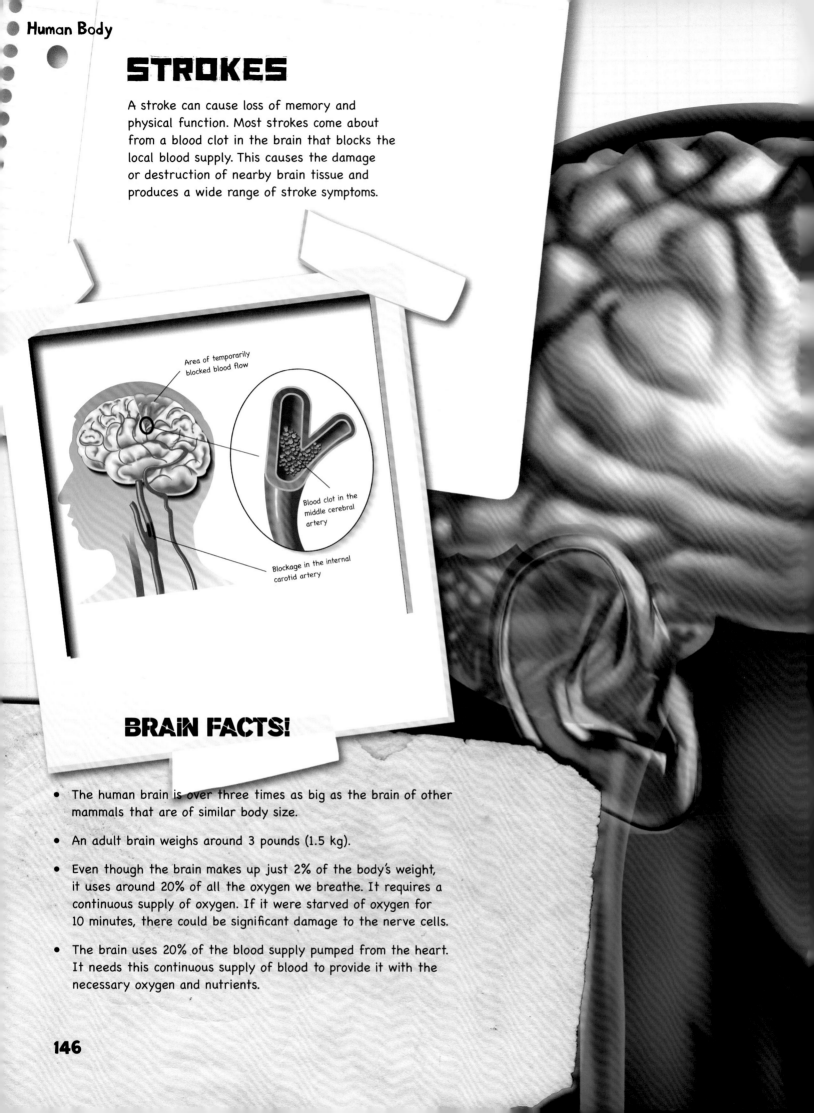

Area of temporarily blocked blood flow

Blood clot in the middle cerebral artery

Blockage in the internal carotid artery

BRAIN FACTS!

- The human brain is over three times as big as the brain of other mammals that are of similar body size.

- An adult brain weighs around 3 pounds (1.5 kg).

- Even though the brain makes up just 2% of the body's weight, it uses around 20% of all the oxygen we breathe. It requires a continuous supply of oxygen. If it were starved of oxygen for 10 minutes, there could be significant damage to the nerve cells.

- The brain uses 20% of the blood supply pumped from the heart. It needs this continuous supply of blood to provide it with the necessary oxygen and nutrients.

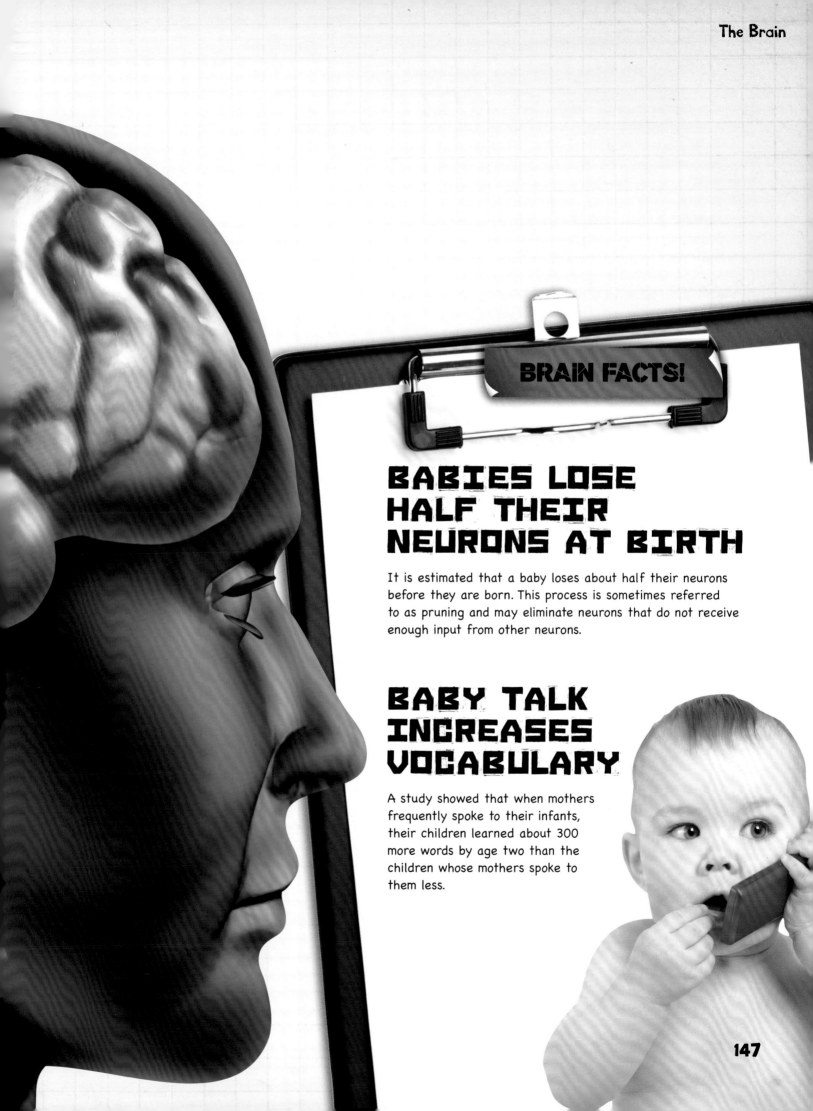

BRAIN FACTS!

BABIES LOSE HALF THEIR NEURONS AT BIRTH

It is estimated that a baby loses about half their neurons before they are born. This process is sometimes referred to as pruning and may eliminate neurons that do not receive enough input from other neurons.

BABY TALK INCREASES VOCABULARY

A study showed that when mothers frequently spoke to their infants, their children learned about 300 more words by age two than the children whose mothers spoke to them less.

SPINAL CORD

The spinal cord works so closely with the brain that you could think of it as a partner of the brain, as they are important to each other. The nervous system is actually broken down further by scientists into two core parts. The spinal cord and the brain together are called the central nervous system, and the rest of the nervous system around the body is called the peripheral nervous system.

The peripheral nervous system has two main types of nerves, called sensory nerves and motor nerves. For example, your sensory nerves react when the skin on your hand touches a hot object and this sends a super-fast message to your brain, which converts to 'Ouch, that's hot!' At the same time, again in super-fast time, your motor nerves immediately send signals to your muscles making your hand move away from the hot object.

DID YOU KNOW?

There are around 100 billion neurons in your body. That's about the same amount as the $100 billion that the gigantic search engine corporation Google was valued at in 2009.

YOU CAN TRY THIS AT HOME!

There are some actions that your body does automatically without needing to send messages through the nervous system to the brain. These actions include blinking, sneezing, shivering, yawning and also your knee reflex.

Why not try this? Sit down and cross one leg over the other. Ask a friend to tap just below your knee. What happens? Your leg should automatically kick upwards and you will not be able to stop it, no matter how hard you try.

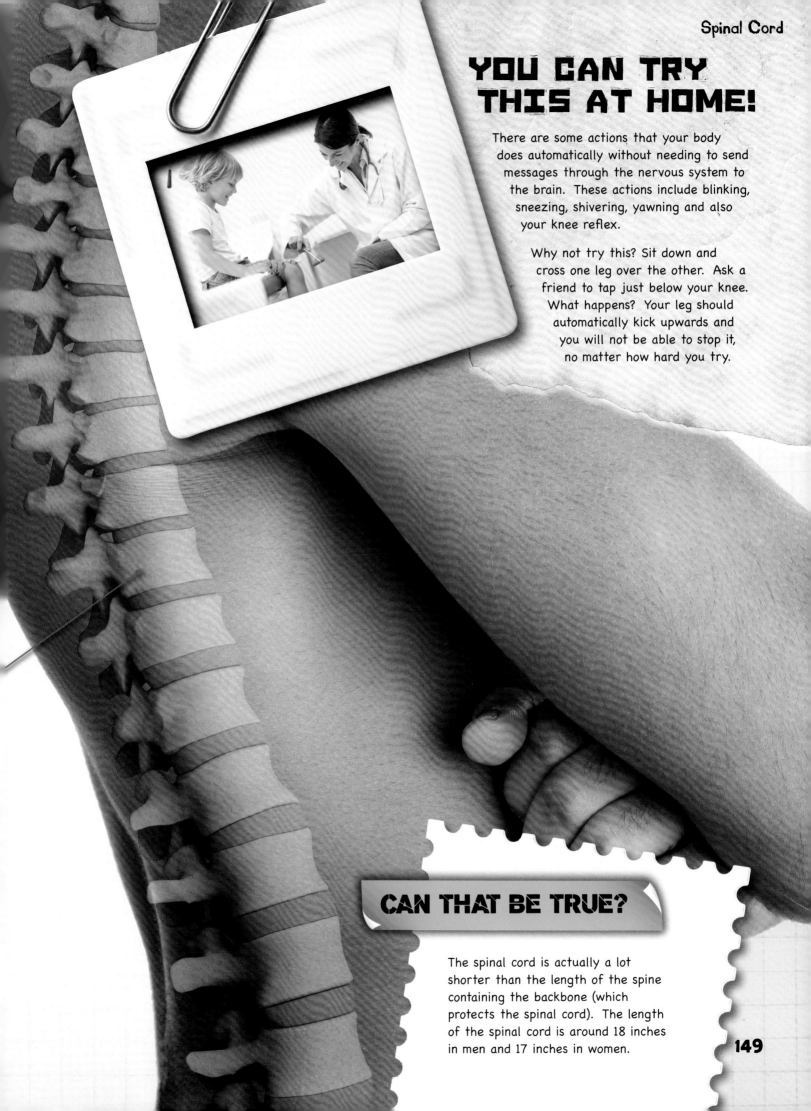

CAN THAT BE TRUE?

The spinal cord is actually a lot shorter than the length of the spine containing the backbone (which protects the spinal cord). The length of the spinal cord is around 18 inches in men and 17 inches in women.

149

THE REPRODUCTIVE SYSTEM

MAKING A BABY

To make a baby there needs to be both a mother and a father. The mother does most of the work during pregnancy but the father has the important role of fertilizing the mother's egg – this is where the father's sperm joins with the mother's egg to create an embryo.

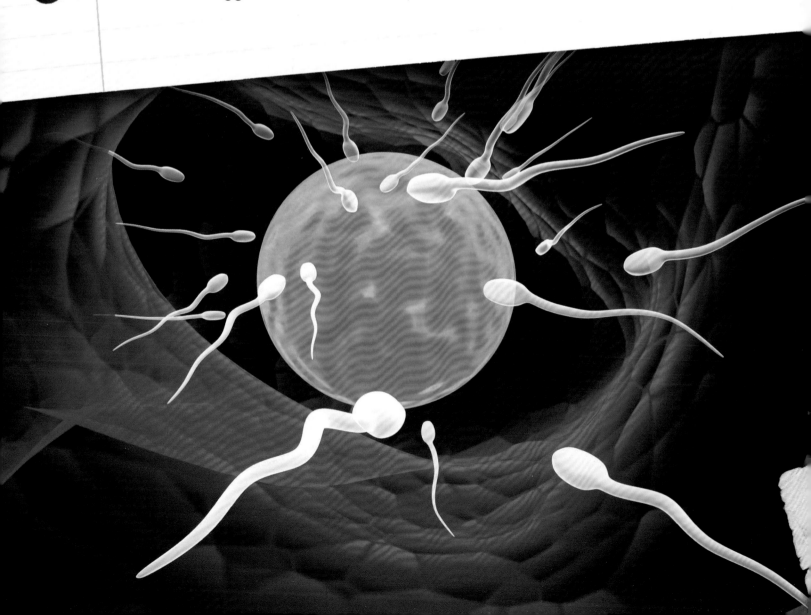

EGGMAZING

A woman's egg is the largest cell in the human body but it is still very tiny, about 1mm in diameter!

SWIMMING GALA

Millions of sperm swim towards the mother's egg cell in a big race to be the first. Only one tadpole-like sperm will bind with the egg to make a new cell and begin a new life.

DID YOU KNOW?

Once the sperm has penetrated the egg, the outer shell becomes impenetrable to other sperm.

HOW COOL!

Male sperm are much smaller than the female eggs, measuring just 3 microns across the head while a fully mature egg is 100 microns in diameter.

DID YOU KNOW?

The average lifespan of an egg after it has left the ovary is 12-24 hours, after which it either disintegrates or is flushed out of the body with the menstrual flow. The average life span of the sperm is 2-3 days.

LET'S SPLIT!

Once the sperm and egg have joined together they then multiply over the coming days.

1 CELL BECOMES 2

By 36 hours the one cell splits and creates an identical copy of itself.

2 BECOMES 4

Over the coming days these cells split again and again, 2 become 4, 4 become 8, 8 become 16.

EMBRYO

After around 3 days there will be an embryo of 16 cells. All of these cells contain instructions on what the baby will look like.

Fertilized egg

2-cell stage

4-cell stage

8-cell stage

16-cell stage

Blastocyst

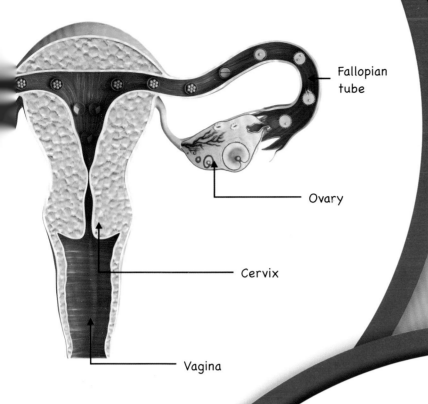

Fallopian
tube

Ovary

Cervix

Vagina

A WARM AND COZY ENVIRONMENT

The uterus or womb is where the baby will grow up and develop during the mother's pregnancy. It is a warm and comfortable place and the embryo (egg) arrives and imbeds into the soft uterus wall after travelling down from a tube called the fallopian tube. It takes about 5 days for the embryo to arrive there after it has started to multiply.

Cleavage

Zygote   2-celled   4-celled   8-celled

Morula

Fusion of egg
and sperm
pronuclei

Blastocyst

Fertilization

Implanted
blastocyst

Ovum

AMAZING!

A woman never runs out of eggs. At birth she has between 1 and 2 million eggs and by puberty has around 350,000 eggs that can be fertilized.

- The arrows indicate the journey of the egg down the fallopian tube.

- Millions of the father's sperm swim up to meet the mother's egg

- After the one sperm and egg have combined they start to travel down the fallopian tube and divide into multiple cells

- At around 5 days the multiple cells (Embryo) attaches itself to the soft yet muscular wall of the uterus and it develops from there into a baby in 40 weeks

GESTATION

A woman becomes pregnant when her egg has been fertilized by the man's sperm and the resulting cell implants itself into the walls of the woman's uterus. From then on, a baby starts to grow inside the woman's womb for around 9 months or 40 weeks. This period of pregnancy is also called **gestation**.

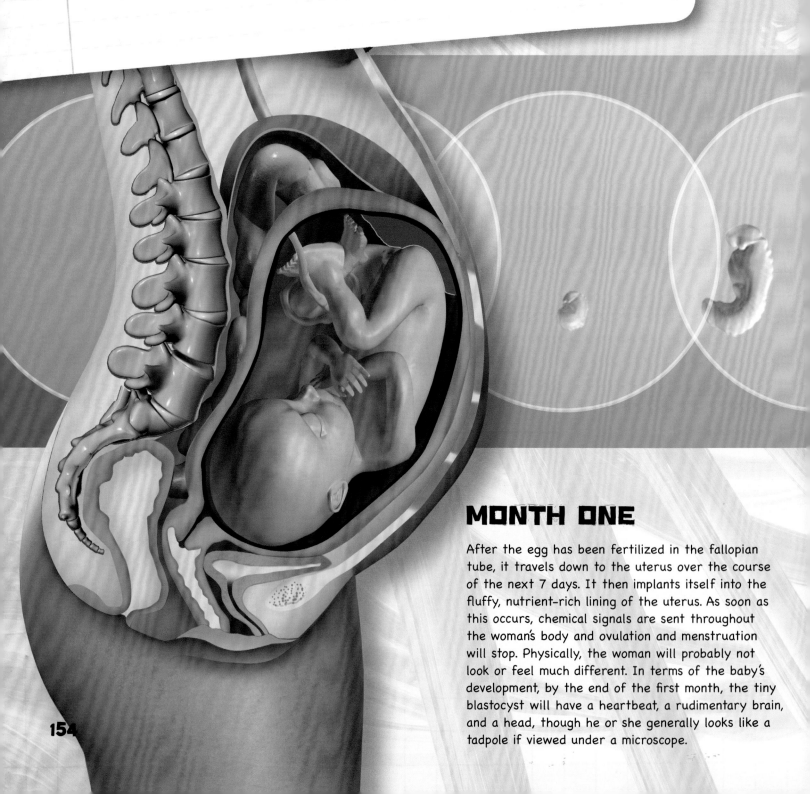

MONTH ONE

After the egg has been fertilized in the fallopian tube, it travels down to the uterus over the course of the next 7 days. It then implants itself into the fluffy, nutrient-rich lining of the uterus. As soon as this occurs, chemical signals are sent throughout the woman's body and ovulation and menstruation will stop. Physically, the woman will probably not look or feel much different. In terms of the baby's development, by the end of the first month, the tiny blastocyst will have a heartbeat, a rudimentary brain, and a head, though he or she generally looks like a tadpole if viewed under a microscope.

154

MONTH TWO

The second month, weeks 5 to 8, is when the mother-to-be starts to feel some of the symptoms of pregnancy. These include fatigue, nausea, headaches, breast changes and more frequent urination. This second month is critical in the development of the baby. Early on in this month the baby develops from a blastocyst into an embryo. It is also the first time their tiny heart starts to beat. By the end of this month, the baby is about an inch (2.5 cm) long and has arms and legs, fingers and toes, as well as the beginning of the major organs such as the liver, pancreas, lungs and stomach.

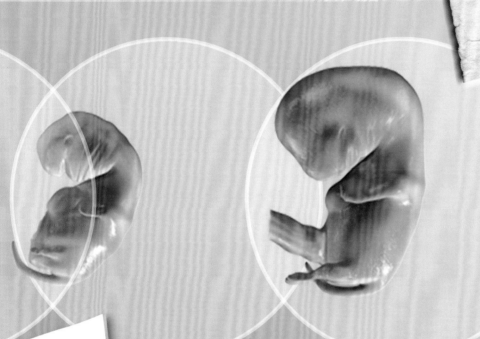

MONTH THREE

During the third month of pregnancy, the baby's bones begin to ossify or harden. The embryo develops into a fetus and it can start to move around. By the end this month, the baby is about the size of an apple and weighs approximately half an ounce (14 grams). The head is about half the size of the body and the brain structure is similar to what it will be at birth. The baby's eyes will be large and open at this stage and ears will also form.

MONTH FOUR

The fetus continues to develop and grow and the expectant mother-to-be may start to feel movement and kicks from the baby. The placenta takes over production of the hormones needed to sustain pregnancy, while the baby is also making some of its own insulin and bile. The baby even urinates into the amniotic fluid in small amounts. It will weigh around 3 ounces (85 grams) and 6.3 inches (16 cm). At this stage the gender may be detectable by ultrasound.

MONTH FIVE

The halfway point of the pregnancy passes during month five, which lasts from around week 18 to week 22. The mother-to-be will most probably appear pregnant and other people may start to notice. While there are no new organ structures forming at this point in pregnancy, the pads of the fingers and toes are developed. This includes creating the baby's fingerprints. The baby is also forming permanent teeth buds behind the baby teeth that are already formed.

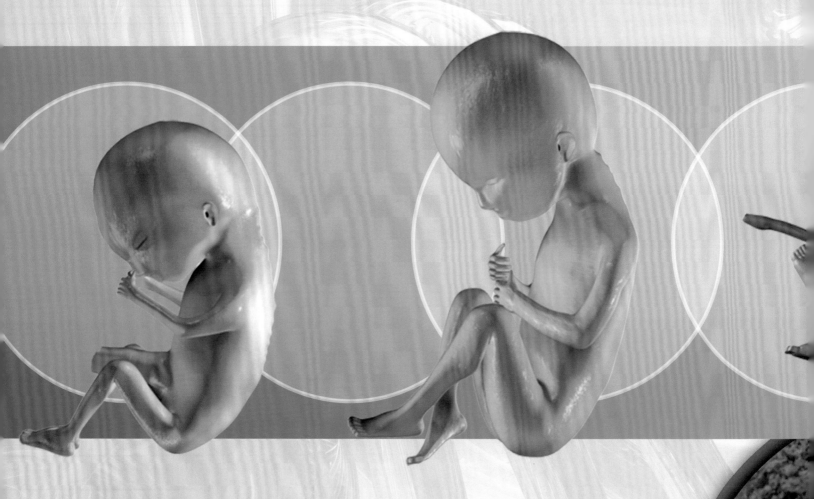

MONTH SIX

From weeks 23 to 27, the baby continues to develop and grow stronger. If the baby is born at this stage it is a premature birth; however, with the advance of medical science there is a fair chance the baby can survive. By the end of this month, eyebrows will have grown and the baby will have started to deposit brown fat. This brown fat will help the baby regulate their body temperature at birth. This brown fat will continue to be laid down until birth. The baby, which weighs around 1 lb 5 ounces (600 grams), is already practicing breathing for when he or she will be born.

MONTH SEVEN

During month 7, the baby's movements change from wild kicks to smaller movements as its growth has taken up most of the space in the uterus. At about week 28, babies begin to start turning their heads to point down automatically, getting ready to be born. The baby's eyelashes are developing and subcutaneous fat is deposited. The baby is about 13.8 inches long (35 cms) and weighs about 2 pounds 4 ounces (1 kilogram).

MONTH EIGHT

During the eighth month, the baby is getting ready to be born. Red blood cell production is done entirely by the baby's bone marrow. The baby's irises can now dilate and contract in response to light. He or she opens and closes their eyes at will. It is during this month that the baby puts on a lot of weight, mostly fat and muscle tissue, and it will now weigh on average 3 lb 11 ounces (1.7 kg) and measure around 15.8 inches (40 cms).

MONTH NINE

The baby's organs have been fully developed for a long time. The baby starts to make final preparations for birth; for example, the lungs secrete a surfactant to help them expand at birth. The baby's kidneys are still producing lots of urine every day, helping to top up the amniotic fluid the baby has been suspended in from the start. The due date given to mothers-to-be by their doctor is a guess as to when the baby may arrive. The majority of babies will be born from two weeks before this date to two weeks after this date. Labor is caused by the baby's signals to the mother's body that he or she is ready to be born. The average birth weight is about 7.5 lbs (3.4 kg) and the baby will measure between 18-22 inches (45-55 cms).

MOVEMENT

Our bodies are ingenious. We can display a huge range of movement from slow, precise and elegant to quick, fast and sometimes not so elegant – Dad dancing!

This movement is powered by our elastic muscles and connected to our strong bones. Our joints too are amazing, the ankle, shoulder, elbow, and wrist all allow us to move our limbs in a variety of ways.

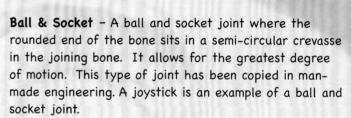

fused joint

JOINT TYPES

Fixed – When you are born you have more individual bones that when you are an adult. For example, your skull is separated into sections, over time these fuse together forming a fixed joint. Once fixed these joints do not move at all.

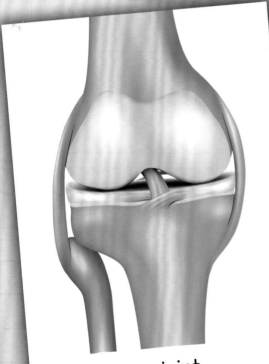

Knee joint

Ball & Socket – A ball and socket joint where the rounded end of the bone sits in a semi-circular crevasse in the joining bone. It allows for the greatest degree of motion. This type of joint has been copied in man-made engineering. A joystick is an example of a ball and socket joint.

Hinge – A hinge joint enables movement in one direction, similar to opening and closing of a hinged door. You have hinged joints in your knee and elbow.

Gliding –This type of joint occurs where you have surfaces of flat bones held together by ligaments. You have these types of joints in your wrist and ankle.

Pivot – Your neck has a pivot joint that allows you to turn your head from side to side.

Saddle – The only saddle joints in your body are in your thumbs. They can rock back and forth and side to side.

SCAN ME
Instructions on page 5

MUSCLES

Bodily movement is powered by muscles all over your body. There are over 600 muscles in your body. They are made up of a stringy elastic material, like a rubber band, which is formed by tens of thousands of small fibers. When an electric signal from your brain stimulates the muscle it contracts, pulling the fibers together and taut. This reduces the length of the muscle and pulls the end of the muscle towards the middle.

You have three different types of muscles in your body, smooth muscle, cardiac muscle and skeletal muscle. It is your skeletal muscle that powers the body in movement. This type of muscle comes in a variety of sizes and shapes. Some of the most powerful and biggest muscles are found in your back helping you stand upright.

Skeletal muscles are attached to bones with tendons. Tendons are strong cords that mean when the muscle contracts and moves it pulls the bone along with it where it is attached.

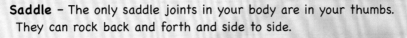

WORKING IN PAIRS

When muscles contract they pull. They cannot push by lengthening out. So to help have full control over the movement, muscles are often in complementary teams. This picture shows a pair of muscles working as a team. These are the biceps and triceps muscles. When the biceps contracts it pulls the forearm up and bends the elbow. To straighten the arm the biceps relaxes and the triceps pulls the forearm down and the arm straightens. This type of muscular team-work occurs all over your body and means that you can quickly straighten and bend your legs and arms.

ROBOTS

Scientists and engineers use our amazing bodies as a blueprint for designing machines. For example, our hollow bone structure has been copied in roll-cages and bicycles to provide maximum strength but minimum weight in comparison to solid metal tubes.

Engineers are studying the human skeletal and muscular system to build robots that can move like us. Robots move in a jolted fashion with quick sharp movements, not the smooth and considered movement we make. This is because it is difficult to engineer something as complex and ingenious as our muscles.

Scientists have managed to develop some artificial limbs that will enable incapacitated people to regain some functionality. These are improving all the time as scientists study the human anatomy and develop further ideas and techniques.

NOT JUST ALL BRAWN

In our very early life, we cannot walk or even crawl. As we grow older and develop we have to learn how to walk and perform more and more complicated movements. These movements build up our muscle and make us better at these movement tasks. Our muscle remembers these movements (muscle memory) and becomes very efficient at them. However, there are some activities that require movements that are not the norm. These require skill and dedication to learn. The brain plays a big part in our motion and pushing the boundaries of what we can achieve.

7 BASIC HUMAN MOVEMENTS

- **Squat** – We squat down to sit down on a chair or kneel with our feet flat on the floor.

- **Run** – We all walk and sometimes run. This is one of the first movements you learn.

- **Push** – We push other people in sports, push open doors and if we exercise and do a push-up we are pushing our body up.

- **Pull** – We pull doors open, if we exercise and do a chin-up we are pulling our body up.

- **Bend** – If we pick something off the floor we bend at the hip and lean over.

- **Twist** – If someone taps you on the shoulder and you look behind you then you are twisting your body to look.

- **Lunge** – When you walk up the stairs you bend your knee and step forwards, this is like lunging forward to hit a low ball in racquet sports.

squat

run

push

pull

bend

twist

lunge

THE PANCREAS

The pancreas is one of our lesser-known organs but you'll be very glad you have one! The pancreas is our control center for using, storing and releasing energy. It is a flat gland around 6 inches long and is found behind your stomach. After you have eaten your breakfast, lunch, dinner, or even a snack, your pancreas goes to work to produce the enzymes that are important for **digestion** and **hormones** that control the sugar in your blood.

The pancreas has two main functions:

1. The first of these is creating special chemicals called **enzymes**. These enzymes travel into the small intestine and produce powerful juices that help digest the food we eat. This food once digested gives us energy to live and grow.

2. The second is creating another kind of special chemicals called **hormones**. Two hormones called insulin and glucagon are created by the beta cells in the pancreas and these special hormones control the amount of sugar in our blood.

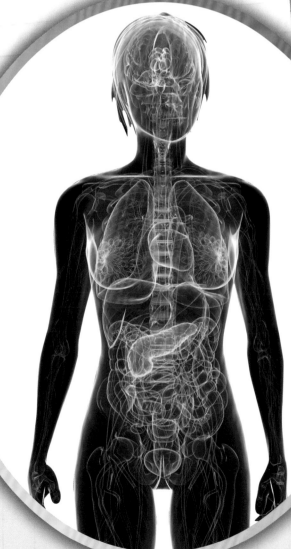

AWESOME

The pancreas is an organ that can be transplanted. If a transplant is successful, a person who was formerly diabetic would no longer have to take insulin or other medication for diabetes.

WHY IS INSULIN IMPORTANT?

If we don't produce enough insulin, sugar cannot be used to fuel our body cells. The cells go into starvation mode and seek other sources of energy such as fat. However, the breakdown of fat leads to the production of harmful substances called ketones, which poison our body.

Lack of insulin is the cause of diabetes, which is a common lifelong health condition. Diabetics need to inject insulin into their bodies to restore the correct insulin levels.

FUN FACT!

Did you know that our pancreas looks a bit like a sweet potato? Sweet potatoes are very good for our pancreas too because they are high in beta-carotene which is an antioxidant. Antioxidants protect the tissues and cells in the body and help restore it from aging and cancer.

IMMUNE SYSTEM

The immune system is your body's self defense system and tries to stop you from getting sick. The system is made up of a combination of cells, organs and tissues.

BODY LININGS

Just like your skin on the outside, the linings of the throat, stomach, intestines and lungs protect you from all of the germs that you ingest and breathe in. Although they are a softer surface than the skin, they are also covered in antibodies called secretory IgA that help kill the germs.

SUPER SKIN

Your skin is super! It is waterproof thanks to an oil secretion called sebum and is also tough. This is your first defense against germs attacking your body. There is bacteria all over your skin and only when you have a cut can they penetrate and potentially infect you.

germs

INTERNAL BATTLE

The main internal defense is germ-fighting cells. These germ-fighting cells are known as white blood cells, also called leukocytes. These cells travel around the bloodstream looking for anything that is not human, such as germs, bacteria and viruses and then attacks and destroys them. They can be found anywhere in the body including the bone marrow, the jelly-like sponge found in large bones.

lymphocytes

Normal Blood

Erythrocytes

Platelets

Neutrophil

Monocyte

Lymphocyte

There are two main types of white blood cells:

Lymphocytes – These are the intelligence corps and the front-line of the cell army. They help the body recognize threats from foreign cells and will remember previous invaders. There are two types of these cells, the B type that recognizes the enemy cell and produces antibodies, and the T type that directly bumps into the foreign invader and kills it.

Phagocytes – Phagocytes do all the dirty work. They clean up all of the dead or dying cells by chewing them up.

165

SPLEEN

The spleen found in your abdomen plays a critical role in the immune system. It filters the blood removing dead or worn out white and red blood cells, making sure your body is fresh to fight infections. There is a concentration of white blood cells found in the spleen.

The Lymphatic System

Cervical lymph nodes

Palatine tonsil

Thymus

Axillary lymph nodes

Right lymphatic duct

Spleen

Thoratic duct

Cisterna chyli

Inguinal lymph nodes

LYMPHATIC SYSTEM

Every army needs a command post and HQ. When an invading pathogen (virus or bacteria) gets past the outer layers of defence, such as the skin, then they must be killed internally. The lymph nodes are the command centres for killing these pathogens. They are located all over your body: on the sides of your neck, under your arms, behind your knees and in your groin. When you are sick and you have 'swollen glands' on your neck, that is actually the lymph node that is swollen and is your immune system hard at work. The lymph node works by filtering out the germs that are brought there by the leukocytes.

IMMUNE SYSTEM PROBLEMS

There are certain medical conditions where your immune system does not work properly. Sometimes instead of fighting pathogens it fights good cells, which can lead to serious damage and illness. Multiple Sclerosis (MS) is one of these illnesses where the immune system attacks its own body.

Allergies are also a problem of an over active immune system. If you are allergic to something the body thinks it is dangerous, even though it is harmless. Many people are allergic to nuts and sometimes the allergy is so serious that it can be fatal.

There are also deceases and viruses that can be contracted which stop the immune system from working, such as HIV/AIDS or Cancer.

NO WAY!!!

IMMUNIZATION

Did you know that sometimes when you get a shot to make you immune to a certain disease or virus (meningitis for example), you are actually given a tiny dose of the disease itself so that your immune system can learn from it should you be infected in the future with more concentration.

CELLS

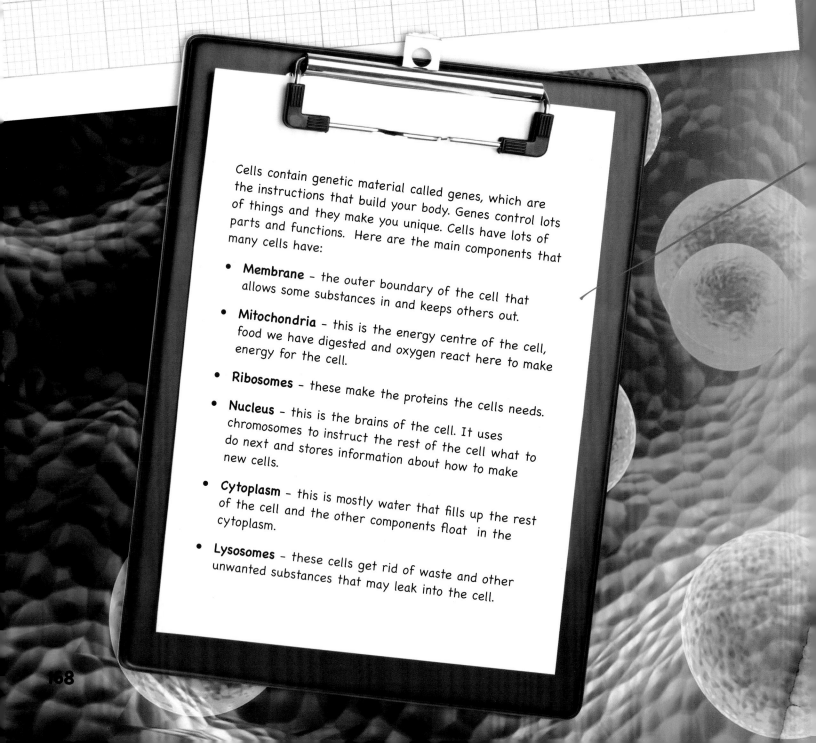

Cells are our body's building blocks and there are around 75 to 100 trillion of them in our bodies. They are in every part of our body and so small that they are invisible to the naked eye. These amazing little cells group together to form a great variety of tissues and all your organs, blood, bones and muscles are made up of these tissues. There are 300 diferent types of cell.

Cells contain genetic material called genes, which are the instructions that build your body. Genes control lots of things and they make you unique. Cells have lots of parts and functions. Here are the main components that many cells have:

- **Membrane** – the outer boundary of the cell that allows some substances in and keeps others out.

- **Mitochondria** – this is the energy centre of the cell, food we have digested and oxygen react here to make energy for the cell.

- **Ribosomes** – these make the proteins the cells needs.

- **Nucleus** – this is the brains of the cell. It uses chromosomes to instruct the rest of the cell what to do next and stores information about how to make new cells.

- **Cytoplasm** – this is mostly water that fills up the rest of the cell and the other components float in the cytoplasm.

- **Lysosomes** – these cells get rid of waste and other unwanted substances that may leak into the cell.

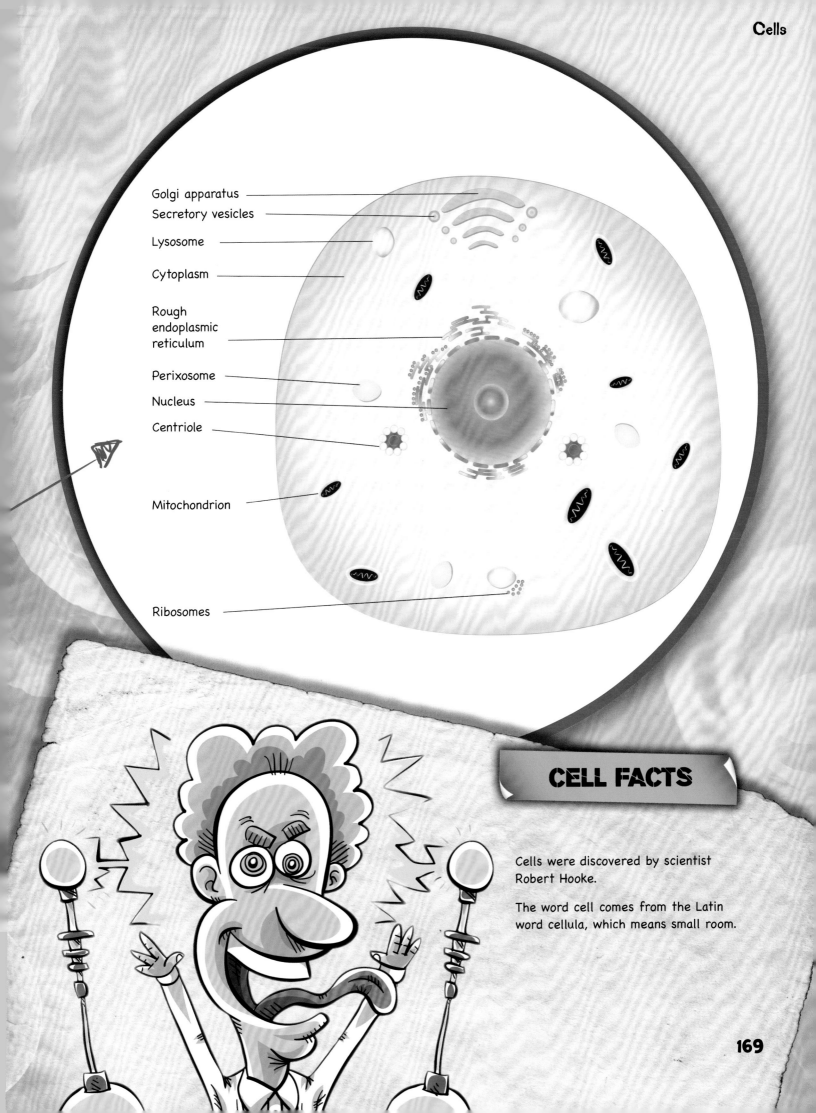

Golgi apparatus

Secretory vesicles

Lysosome

Cytoplasm

Rough
endoplasmic
reticulum

Perixosome

Nucleus

Centriole

Mitochondrion

Ribosomes

CELL FACTS

Cells were discovered by scientist
Robert Hooke.

The word cell comes from the Latin
word cellula, which means small room.

There are more bacterial cells in the body than human cells. Scientists estimate that about 95% of all the cells in the body are actually bacteria. Most of these **bacteria** cells are in the **digestive tract**.

MAKING NEW CELLS

Cells are constantly reproducing themselves. Amazingly, millions of them die and are replaced every second. To do this, they divide in two and the new cells are half the size of the original, although they soon grow. While you were reading this page you probably lost over 2000 dead skin cells!

HOW LONG DO CELLS LIVE?

Cells have varying life spans, from a few days to up to a year. Certain cells of the digestive tract live for a few days, while some **immune system** cells can live for up to six weeks. Pancreatic cells can live for as long as a year.

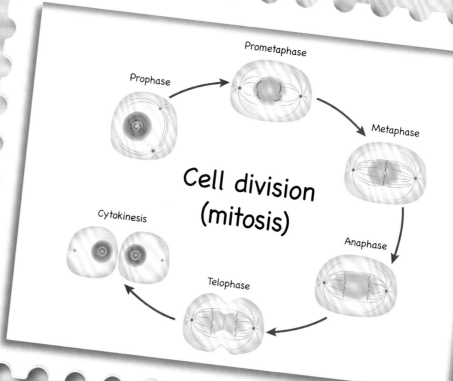

Prophase
Prometaphase
Metaphase
Cell division (mitosis)
Anaphase
Cytokinesis
Telophase

WHAT ARE ORGANELLES?

Cells contain structures called organelles which carry out specific functions. Organelles have a huge range of responsibilities within each cell these include things like providing energy and producing hormones and enzymes.

ALL TOO MUCH!

Cells can commit suicide. When a cell becomes damaged or undergoes some type of infection, it will self destruct.

DID YOU KNOW?

Our bodies have special germ-killing cells released lby the immune system to fight off infection.

BIG AND SMALL

The tiniest cell in your body is a very, very small brain cell that helps to detect different types of smell. The biggest are the egg cells in a woman's body. They are still very small, around 1mm, and you would still need quite a lot of them to make up the size of a grain of rice.

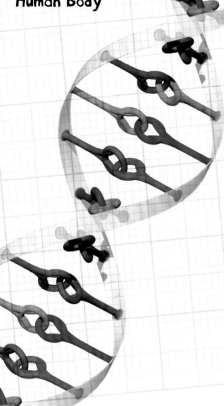

DNA

DNA, short for deoxyribonucleic acid, is our body's instructions for life and is contained inside billions of our cells, it is wickedly complicated! DNA is inherited by children from each parent, which is why families share traits like skin, hair and eye color. It looks like a curved ladder which is called a double helix.

The main function of DNA is to tell each cell what to do, rather like a boss! It sends a series of instructions a bit like computer code, this code is made up of four parts or bases which make up the rungs in the DNA ladder.

A - Adenine   T - Thymine   C - Cytosine   G - Guanine

These bases always pair up together, however they are a bit choosey about pairing up. The simplest way to look at it is:-

A and T are best buddies and always need to hang out together

G and C are also best buddies and need to hang out together

The pairs can come in any order to make up the instruction code. Each piece of code tells our cells to make a protein and these proteins help each cell to do its job.

172

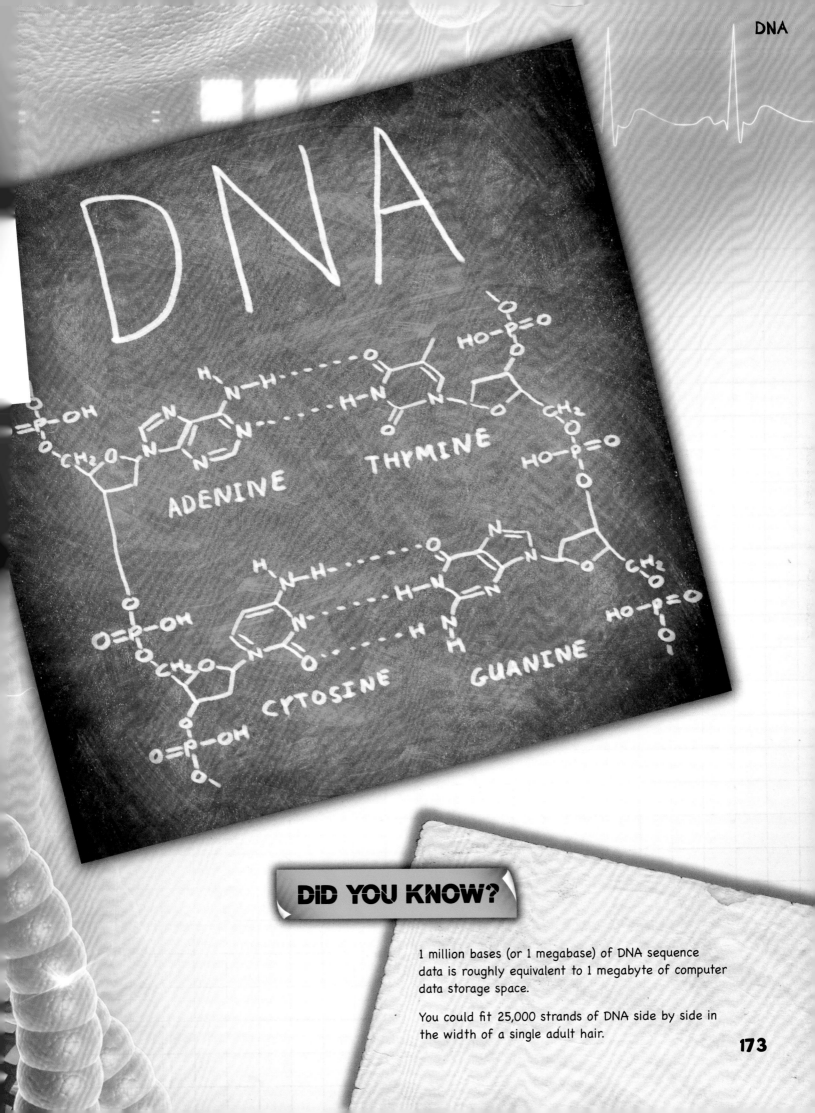

DID YOU KNOW?

1 million bases (or 1 megabase) of DNA sequence data is roughly equivalent to 1 megabyte of computer data storage space.

You could fit 25,000 strands of DNA side by side in the width of a single adult hair.

DNA TESTING

DNA is a powerful tool for identifying people. Testing is done by singling out the genetic markers within the code, these are the bits that make us unique. Two samples will be used to test against each other for matches.

DNA testing is used for lots of things but the most well known are:-

Parental testing – to find out a child's biological parents.

Forensic testing – to identify suspects in a crime.

Gene therapy – to test for genetic conditions or birth defects during pregnancy.

Genetic genealogy – to find out about our ancestors.

All cells within the body contain exactly the same DNA so testing samples can be taken from almost anywhere, most commonly though hair follicles, skin, blood and other bodily fluids are used.

DNA testing has been around since the mid-to-late 1980s, but it was not perfected until the late 1990s. Test results used to take over a week to come in but recently due to improvements in technology test results can come back in minutes. DNA helps catch many criminals on a daily basis.

Timothy Wilson Spencer was the first man in the US to be sentenced to death due to DNA evidence.

When Anna Anderson famously claimed to be the Grand Duchess Anastasia, a member of the Russian royal family, DNA busted her. The tests after she died showed she wasn't related at all! The DNA tests for the O. J. Simpson case were the most famous early use of DNA evidence.

YOU'RE BUSTED!

FUN FACTS ABOUT DNA

Our DNA is 98 per cent the same as chimpanzees and 50 per cent the same as bananas!

The only cells in the human body that do not contain DNA are red blood cells.

If all the DNA in the human body were unwound, it would reach to the moon and back 6,000 times.

WHO DISCOVERED DNA?

DNA was first isolated and recognized as a unique form by Friedrich Miescher in 1869, but it wasn't until 1953 that James D. Watson and Francis Crick suggested what is now accepted as the first correct double-helix model of DNA structure which was published in the journal Nature. They won a Nobel prize for their work.

THE GENOME

The human genome holds the key to who we are and how our bodies work, it's like a complicated bit of encrypted code that scientists are currently trying to crack. A genome is the inherited genetic material that governs the development of the human body, it is much like a blueprint describing how we should be built. Every person is made up of parts of both of their parents, there is so much information available that what we inherit isn't always seen even though it is there. There are between 26,000 and 40,000 genes in the human body. Our genomes are contained in chromosomes and chromosomes store genetic information known as DNA in a cell.

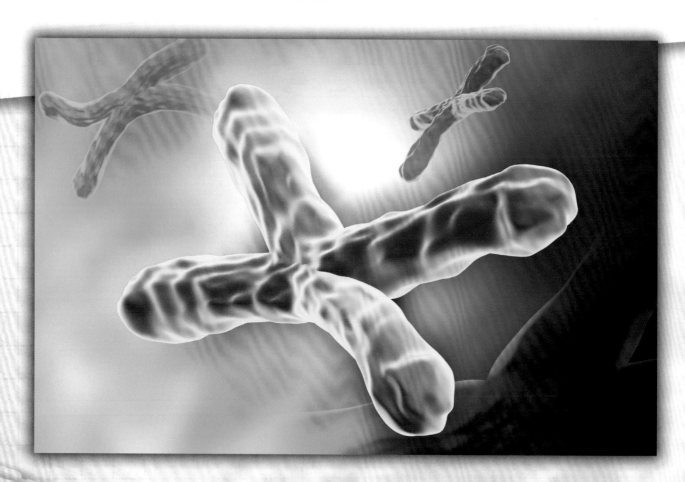

WHAT ARE CHROMOSOMES?

Chromosomes are like the filing cabinets for all our genetic information. They are inherited from our parents and they contain two tightly coiled strands of DNA that join in the middle to form an x shape. They are thread-like strands that contain hundreds, or even thousands, of genes. Most people have 23 pairs of chromosomes, you receive half from your mother and the other half from your father.

WHAT ARE GENETIC DISORDERS?

A genetic disorder is caused by an abnormality within an individual's DNA. These abnormalities can range from a small mutation in a single gene to entire chromosomes, or segments of them, which are missing, duplicated, or otherwise altered.

Sickle cell disease is a disorder that is caused by a faulty gene. It affects the red blood cells, which transport oxygen from the lungs to the rest of the body. Normally, red blood cells are round and flexible so they can travel freely through the narrow blood vessels, however sickle cells are crescent-shaped which causes lots of problems with oxygen supply.

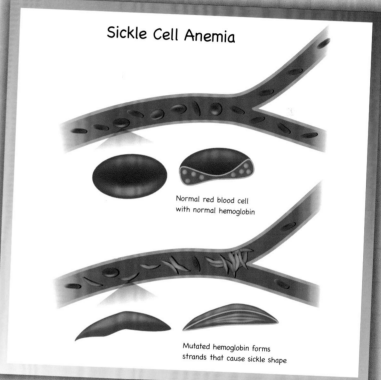

Sickle Cell Anemia

Normal red blood cell with normal hemoglobin

Mutated hemoglobin forms strands that cause sickle shape

In rare cases, some people are born with an extra chromosome. People born with an extra chromosome 21, for example, have Down's syndrome.

Scientists know now which genes cause some genetic disorders and one day they may be able to replace damaged genes or cure genetic diseases.

DOLLY THE SHEEP

Scientists have the power to manipulate and reproduce genes using genetic engineering. In 1996, scientists successfully cloned a sheep which was known as Dolly. Cloning is the creation of an organism that is an exact genetic copy of another. This means that every single bit of DNA is the same between the two! Dolly died in 2003 from lung disease and sparked a lot of debate around the whole idea about the ethics of cloning.

FUN FACT

It takes about 8 hours for one of your cells to completely copy its DNA.

TWINS

Twins are the natural human version of cloning. Identical twins are formed if a fertilized human embryo splits into two. Identical twins share the same genetic information because they come from the same embryo.

GM FOODS

Scientists can also change the genes in food. This is called genetic modification, and is a way of speeding up the process of selection by breeding. Food crops have their genes modified to enhance taste and quality, or improve resistance to pests and disease. In some cases, GM foods help conserve natural resources, for instance the altered version might require less watering. There is still much to be learnt about genetic modification and the whole subject is a political hot potato!

DID YOU KNOW?

The first genetically modified food to reach our tables was the Flavr Savr tomato.

MAPPING THE HUMAN GENOME

The Human Genome Project, was an international project designed to discover the exact makeup of the genetic material that controls the way human beings develop and grow. Scientists from all over the world worked together on this project which started in 1990 and was completed in 2003.

Discovering the secrets of this highly complex code is still in its infancy. Scientists now know the position of some of the genes that control our medical traits but there is still a lot of information we do not know about other genes. Cracking the human genome is very important as it will give us a better understanding about how life works and it could lead to preventing or curing diseases.

GENOME FACT

The study of the human genome is called genomics and it is used to study many different things. The most common of these are:-

- Evolution

- What causes a disease

- New medical treatments

FUN FACT

The human genome is made up of 3 billion bases of DNA, split into 23 chromosomes. The information contained in these bases would fill 200 500-page telephone directories and would take a century to recite, if recited at one letter per second for 24 hours a day!

179

DIET

YOU ARE WHAT YOU EAT

It is true when people say you are what you eat. Food can be something artistic and eccentric, it can be a treat and it makes us feel good when we eat something very tasty. Food can also be functional, boring and bland. It may not taste good but it serves its purpose of feeding the body. Food is where we get our fuel to provide us with energy. It is also how we get the nutrients, vitamins and minerals essential for our body. Our diet is what we eat and a good diet is necessary for a healthy body. A good diet includes a mix of carbohydrates, fats, vitamins, minerals, proteins, fiber and water in the correct amounts.

FOOD PYRAMID

The above food pyramid demonstrates a good diet of the different types of food available. At the top, with the least space, there are sweets and sugar-filled treats. These are the foods that you should have rarely. As you go down the pyramid, the areas with more space contain foods that you should have more of in your diet. Below sweets are dairy products (milk, cheese) and meats and fish. Below this are fruit and vegetables and at the bottom, the main part of our diet should consist of carbohydrates, such as bread, grain and rice.

Fuel – Your body needs fuel and this is mostly provided by carbohydrates. This is why carbohydrates feature in the largest portion of your diet in the food pyramid.

Fats – Fats can provide some fuel to the body but they come from greasy foods and they do not dissolve in water. Examples include solid fats in meat and cheese as well as liquid fats like cooking oil. These fats are not usually burned or used immediately after consumption so are stored throughout the body until they are needed.

Proteins – Proteins are a very important part of your diet. Proteins are made by amino acids and are used to build muscle as well as to create and repair cells. Proteins are found in meats and fish but also nuts and certain seeds.

Fiber – Fiber is also a very important part of your diet but many people forget about it as your body cannot digest it. Fiber is necessary to keep the digestive system healthy and the muscles in the bowel exercised.

BELLA ITALIA

In Italy and many other Mediterranean countries, such as Greece, the diet consists of lots of fruit, vegetables, fish and olive oil. This Mediterranean diet is considered to be very healthy.

EXERCISE

Everyone needs to exercise in order to keep their body fit and healthy on both the outside and the inside. Exercise can be anything from playing a sport, going to the gym, taking a walk or even gardening. People exercise for various reasons but mainly because they enjoy it, it keeps them fit and it helps them lose weight. During exercise, your muscles are working much more than normal so require more fuel. This fuel is oxygen and glucose (sugar) and they are provided by blood. This means that when you exercise, your heart has to work harder too. It can beat twice as fast and pump twice as much blood to the muscles. The blood can be boosted with ten times more oxygen than normal from fast and deep breathing. Meanwhile, the extra glucose is released into the blood from the liver by the hormone adrenalin.

DON'T CRAMP MY STYLE

Cramp is caused by a lack of oxygen to the muscles which then fill up with painful lactic acid as a result. One of the ways to relieve this is to massage the cramped area to release the lactic acid.

MENTAL FITNESS

Did you know that regular exercise has been proven to boost 'feeling good' hormones such as serotonin (chocolate also has this effect) and can help avoid feeling down and blue.

WARMING UP AND COOLING DOWN

When undertaking any exercise, you should warm up before you start and cool down when you have finished. This means stretching out the muscles you are going to use and getting them ready for a workout. After exercise, stretching those muscles used will help reduce cramp from any lactic acid build up, but also relax the muscles from tensing too hard.

GYM

The gym can be used for everything from running and cycling to taking exercise classes such as yoga. However, most people associate the gym with building muscles. You can use weights to build up your muscles by steadily increasing over time the amount of weight you use on a specific muscle group. It is important, however, to ask for expert advice on training with weights as they can damage your muscles if not used properly. Generally gyms only allow adults to use the weights and weight machines for health and safety reasons.

YOGA

Yoga is a discipline of exercise originating from ancient India. The main purpose of yoga is to stretch your body and move it into positions that gently Stretch certain muscles. This not only helps with flexibility but also muscle toning and strength. Some people also suggest that the spirituality of yoga combined with the gentle physical exertion provides them with a sense of relaxation afterwards.

RUNNING

Running is by far the most common exercise people undertake. It is also free and enjoyable. Some people train in running in short sprints, which is suggested to burn (use) more calories, while others go for long runs of 5 or 10 miles (8 to 16 km). Either way, it is important to wear proper running shoes to protect your feet and joints, especially if running on asphalt (tarmac).

FIT AND FACTY

- Exercise makes you feel more energized because it releases endorphins into the blood.
- On average, a person walks 70,000 miles (112,000 km) in their lifetime.
- The only exercise you should hold your breath for is underwater swimming.
- The heart is the strongest muscle in the body.
- Nearly 55% of all young people aged 12 to 21 are not vigorously active on a daily basis.
- For every pound of muscle gained, the body burns 50 extra calories every day.
- Only 15% of men are physically fit.
- More than 35% of children aged 6-11 are overweight, and over 17% are obese.

183

GROWTH AND DEVELOPMENT

The human life cycle has 6 stages that we all pass through unless of course we die prematurely. Hormones pay a major role in how our body changes over our lifetime and our DNA already has a plan laid out for how we are going to look. Over the centuries thanks to human progress, particularly with respect to healthcare and medicine, we are living longer than ever before. The life expectancy of someone in an industrialized country such as the USA, UK and Germany is around 70 years old.

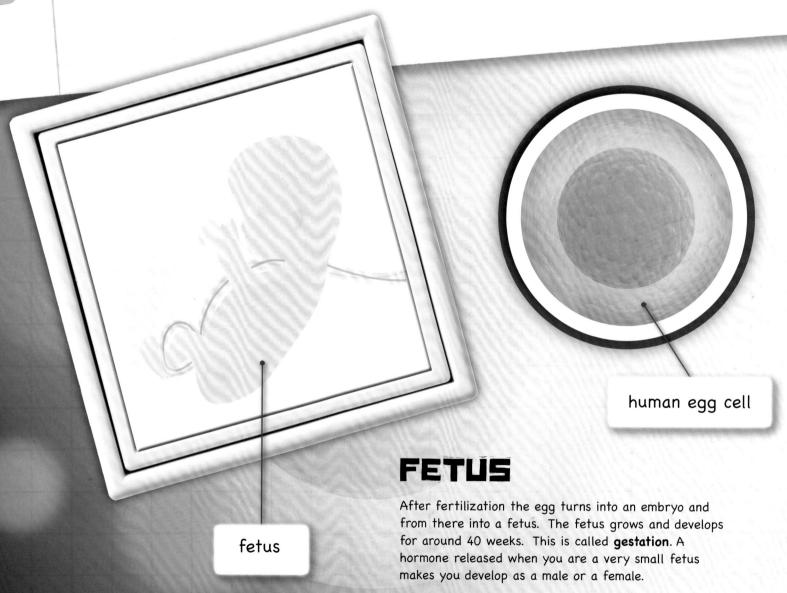

fetus

human egg cell

FETUS

After fertilization the egg turns into an embryo and from there into a fetus. The fetus grows and develops for around 40 weeks. This is called **gestation**. A hormone released when you are a very small fetus makes you develop as a male or a female.

BABY

When you are born you immediately take your first breath and life in the open world begins. A baby's body is still under developed, you have more bones than you will ever have and they are soft and flexible. Your skull is separated into parts and you are dependent on your parents to feed and clean you.

CHILDHOOD

As you grow from a baby into a toddler and enter childhood you grow at a rapid rate. You turn all the food you eat into energy but also into body tissue like muscles. Calcium is also very important to help you grow strong bones, which are made of calcium, so that is why mom always asked you to drink your milk!

185

ADOLESCENCE

From around the age of 10–16 there will be another rapid growth stage that is triggered by the onset of puberty. Hormones are responsible for this and they make your body change and prepare you for reproduction at a later stage in your life. Girls turn into women, they develop breasts and start their menstruation cycle. Boys turn into men, their voice lowers and they grow, becoming stronger with much bigger muscles.

ADULTHOOD

After adolescence when your body has completed the growth caused by puberty, usually at age 18-25, you become a fully grown adult. Your body will not grow any further but there will be changes as the 'wear and tear' of the years go by and your body starts to age. There is scientific evidence to suggest your brain keeps on developing until you are in your 40s.

OLD AGE

This is the last stage of life. As you become old a lack of certain hormones starts the process of slowly shutting the body down. Bones become more brittle and easy to break, they even shrink a little. Muscles become weaker and for most people their hair will lose its color and become gray. They may even lose lots of their hair. For women they will also stop their menstrual cycle, this is called the **menopause**. Women do, on average, tend to live longer than men so they have a longer old age stage.

LIFE EXPECTANCY

Look at these graphs of life expectancy, we are living longer now than we ever have before.

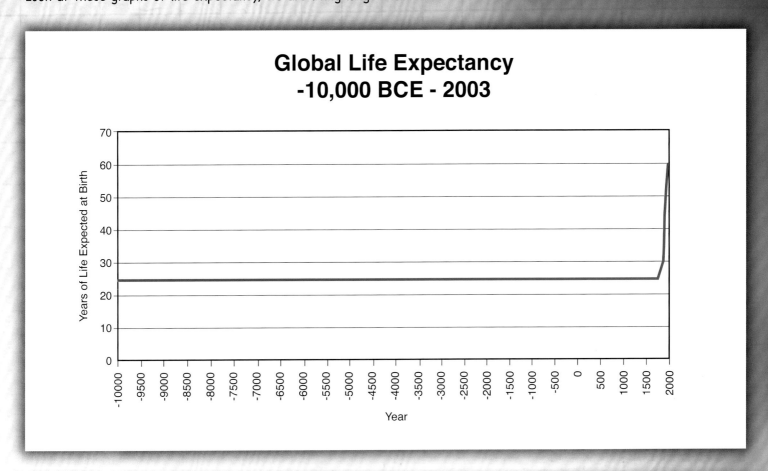

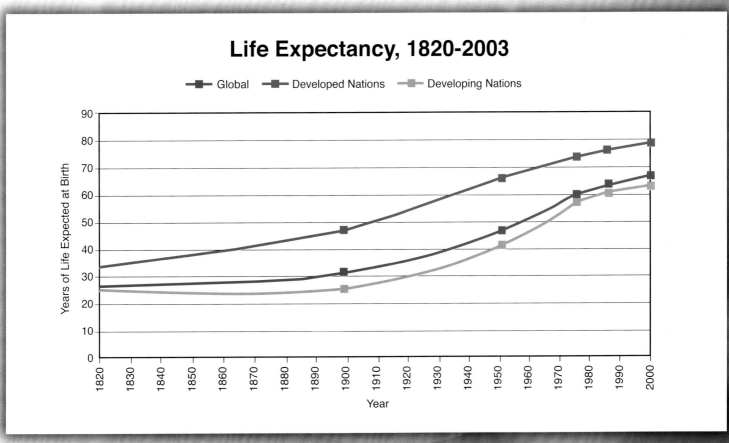

HUMAN EVOLUTION

Humans are very special, not just because of our extraordinary brains and intelligence but, like other life forms, we are made up of complex chemical reactions, biological processes and systems all encased within a physical, dynamic structure.

What we look like (for example, body shape, size, hair color) is all determined by our genes. All of this information is coded in our DNA, which instructs our body on how to grow. Our DNA is made up of half of our mother's DNA and half of our father's.

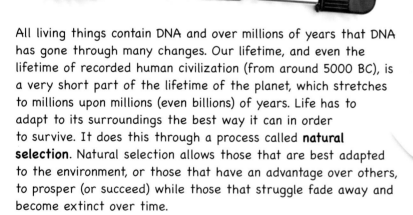

All living things contain DNA and over millions of years that DNA has gone through many changes. Our lifetime, and even the lifetime of recorded human civilization (from around 5000 BC), is a very short part of the lifetime of the planet, which stretches to millions upon millions (even billions) of years. Life has to adapt to its surroundings the best way it can in order to survive. It does this through a process called **natural selection**. Natural selection allows those that are best adapted to the environment, or those that have an advantage over others, to prosper (or succeed) while those that struggle fade away and become extinct over time.

This process is brought about by the occasional mutation (or change) of DNA. This change can be beneficial, harmful or neutral. If it is beneficial, then it is likely that the offspring (or children) will inherit this change and will prosper and have further offspring. Through reproduction over time, the beneficial change spreads so that the change then becomes the norm (or normal). Over a long period of time, this can cause new species to form. This whole process is known as **evolution**.

WE'RE LIKE MOTORCARS??

A simple yet useful analogy (or comparison) of evolution is the development of motorcars. They started as very simple machines – the first motorcar only had one gear! Over time, as engineers have added pieces onto the car and re-designed other parts, some of these adaptations have become the norm as they made the car better, for example, more fuel efficient, faster, or more durable (or longer-lasting). No one adaptation is better than the other, as it depends on what the car is designed to do. Is it in a race? Then faster is better. Is it a commuter car? Then fuel efficiency is important. Or is it a rental car? In this case, durability is the best. There are other factors that make the car better as well, such as looks, brand, sound and more. However, one thing is certain, there will be aspects that still survive directly or indirectly from the original motorcar. A great example of this is wheels! They may have been modified, but they are still a consistent and unchanging feature on all cars.

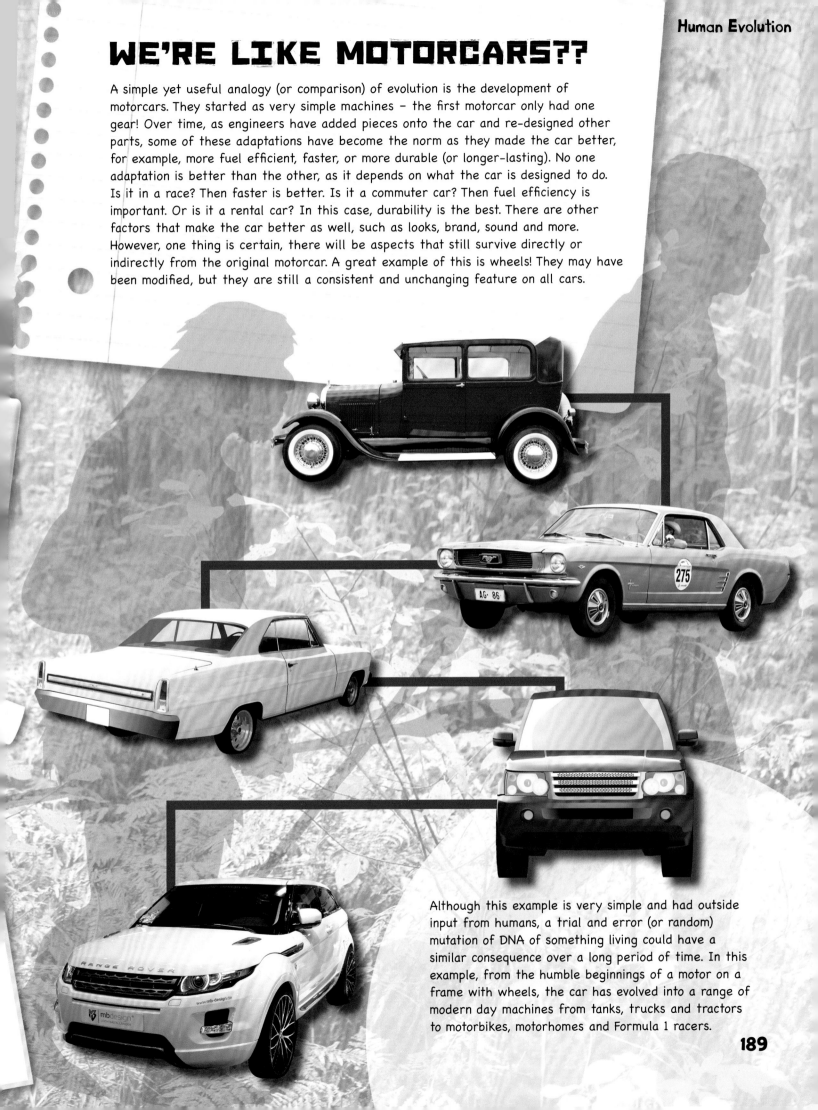

Although this example is very simple and had outside input from humans, a trial and error (or random) mutation of DNA of something living could have a similar consequence over a long period of time. In this example, from the humble beginnings of a motor on a frame with wheels, the car has evolved into a range of modern day machines from tanks, trucks and tractors to motorbikes, motorhomes and Formula 1 racers.

LIFE THEORY

According to the theory of evolution, chemicals randomly organized themselves into a self-replicating (or reproducing) molecule. This replication went through mutations over a significant time period and is the basis of every living thing that has ever existed on our planet.

SHERLOCK, WHERE'S THE EVIDENCE FOR EVOLUTION?

The theory of evolution is based on clues found in the ancient remains of animals. These were fossilized over millions of years and show that some of the characteristics of animals living today are shared with those in the fossils. Some of the fossils contained characteristics that are not present now and so they must have become extinct. Dinosaurs are a good example of this, although some of the dinosaurs share characteristics with modern-day birds.

CHARLES DARWIN 1809 – 1882

Charles Darwin was an English naturalist who formed the theory of evolution after studying the animals and plants he saw on a trip around the world between 1831 and 1836. In 1859, he published his theories in On the Origin of Species although many scientists and the Church denied the evidence at the time. Since then, science has proved many of his theories, particularly with the discovery of DNA and the genome code.

FACT

Your brother is a chimp! Read the 'Did you know?' below to find out why.

MONKEY BUSINESS

Humans evolved from ape-like creatures that lived in Africa around 5 million years ago. Early humans left the dense forests for more open woodlands and grassy plains and evolved new features. One of these features was the ability to walk upright. This enabled early humans to use their hands more, pick up objects and start to use tools. With the greater height from standing up (bipedal), they were also able to survey their surroundings and look out for prey or enemies. All these new abilities helped develop the brain further, which led to the evolution of larger brains with more skills such as thinking, planning and communication. Meanwhile the apes and monkeys that stayed in the dense forest evolved but not as drastically as we have.

DID YOU KNOW?

Did you know that our DNA is 97% the same as that of chimpanzees? We are also 96% the same as gorillas!

HUMAN DISEASES

Although our bodies are fantastic at keeping us going and keeping us healthy, unfortunately people can sometimes be affected by serious sickness, or disease. As a human race, we spend a lot of time researching the causes of certain life-changing diseases so that we can fight them and everyone can benefit. Diseases can be caught through no fault of our own, but there are also a number of ways to try to avoid catching some of the really horrible ones. The diseases listed on these pages are only a few of the many harmful sicknesses out there.

AiDS

AIDS stands for acquired immunodeficiency syndrome. AIDS is caused by the virus HIV (human immunodeficiency virus). The virus attacks the body's immune system so that it cannot protect itself from infections. Someone who has contracted HIV may not have the full effects of the disease until much later on. Medicine is progressing to prevent HIV affecting the immune system so that the actual disease AIDS does not result. Once the disease AIDS has been diagnosed, even a common cold could kill the person infected. HIV is contracted through blood (for example, when drug users share needles) and sexual contact.

CANCER

Cancer is unfortunately a common disease. It is when the cells that grow and divide start to grow out of control. Usually when cells grow, they know when to stop. However, cancerous cells continue to divide and grow. They usually form clusters, making a tumor. These cancerous cells can damage the healthy cells and tissue and then even spread to other parts of the body. Cancer is not contagious, meaning you cannot catch it from another person. Scientists are still unsure why some people develop cancer but there is strong evidence suggesting that certain activities, such as smoking, can cause cancer.

INFLUENZA

Influenza is more commonly known as the flu. It is a virus that infects you and can cause a fever, sinus problems, aches in the body, headaches and a cough. As it is caused by a virus and not a bacteria, standard antibiotics will not work to beat it. You can catch the flu from other people and the best ways to avoid catching it or passing it on are by washing your hands and covering your mouth when you cough. For those vulnerable to infection whose immune system is quite weak, for example the elderly or very young children, there is a flu vaccine (or flu shot) available.

193

THE PLAGUE

The plague is from a bacterial infection that causes a horrific illness, where the body breaks out in pus-filled blisters and you cough blood before eventually dying. In medieval Europe, the infamous 'Black Death' was the plague that swept across Europe in the 1340s and killed an estimated 25 million people. The plague is spread by fleas found on rodents such as rats. The fleas jump onto humans and infect them by biting them and sucking their blood. Fortunately, the plague has been wiped out for most of the world, mainly due to cleanliness but also thanks to modern medicine. It does still exist in some small areas in very poor countries where medicine to combat it is not available.

EWW, GROSS!

Doctors used to believe that bad smells would drive away the plague, so some of the treatments used contained animal dung (or feces) and urine. Of course, it probably made the patient worse and would have been more likely to help spread the disease than prevent it.

SMALLPOX

Smallpox is a very serious illness that, thanks to the progress of medicine, has been eradicated (destroyed completely). There has not been a diagnosis of smallpox in the world since 1977. However, it does still exist in some special, well-protected laboratories for scientists to study. Smallpox is caused by the variola virus and leads to pus-filled blisters all over your body and can eventually lead to death. It is a virus that is very contagious and is spread just like the flu.

MALARIA

Malaria is an infection from a parasite and can cause fevers and death. It is treatable and even preventable with certain medicine. However, many people still die as a result of contracting malaria because they live in poor and remote places around the world. Around 200-300 million people are infected with malaria each year. Malaria is spread by mosquitoes so it is usually only found in hot tropical environments such as sub-Saharan Africa, where around 2 million people die each year.

DID YOU KNOW?

Malaria is passed on by a mosquito biting a person already infected with the disease and then carrying the parasite that causes the disease to the next person they bite. Only female mosquitoes actually bite, so it is only the female ones that can transmit malaria.

FUN FACT

Smallpox was the first disease ever to be eradicated worldwide. The first vaccine (a shot you have to prevent you getting a disease) for small pox was created as far back as 1796. In England, a doctor called Edward Jenner noticed that cows had a similar, but much less serious, disease called cowpox and he used that to create a vaccine to prevent people from getting smallpox.

PARASITES, VIRUSES AND BACTERIA

PARASITES

Parasites are organisms that derive nourishment and protection from other living organisms known as hosts. Parasites have a close relationship with their host but as they use them ultimately to extract food, this process generally harms the host, and may even kill it. They can also use a host to multiply and, especially with parasitic insects, there can be horrific consequences as the host can be eaten away from the inside. Parasites can either live on the surface of the host, for example a blood sucking flea, or inside it like tapeworms. There are examples of parasites in both the plant and animal kingdoms and some fairly gruesome fungi.

HOOK WORM

A very well-known and common parasite the hookworm. It is possible for humans or their pets to get them. Hookworms attach themselves in the lining of the small intestine, and cause diseases, and malnutrition as well, as they eat the nutrients and keep them from going to the host. Millions of Americans have intestinal parasites. This usually does not cause too much of a medical problem but for people with weakened immune systems, such as people with HIV, intestinal parasites can be very serious and even life threatening.

BACTERIA

Bacteria are everywhere, they are on your skin, in the food you eat, on the book you are reading right now, they are even inside you. They are considered to be the smallest and simplest of living creatures. They are very simple cells that fall under the heading prokaryotic. Prokaryotic means that the bacteria do not have an organized nucleus. Bacteria are small single cells whose whole purpose in life is to replicate. While they do not have an organized nucleus, they do have DNA, cell membranes and a protective cell wall like any other cell.

Do not let the fact that they are so small and simplistic make you think that bacteria do not have a variety of functions. They do all sorts of things; some cause diseases, some break down usually inedible food in the stomachs of animals, and some are in modern medicines that we use to fight other bacteria. There are millions of types of both good and bad bacteria.

There are three usual shapes that bacteria form:

Spherical bacteria are in the shape of little spheres or balls. They usually form chains of cells like a row of circles.

Rod shaped bacteria look like the E. coli living in your intestine. They can make chains like a set of linked sausages.

Spiral shaped bacteria twist to form a corkscrew-like shape.

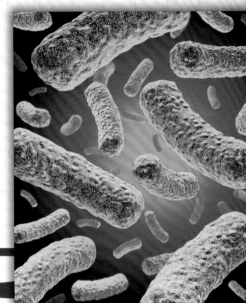

BACTERIA FACTS

Bacteria can live anywhere, even in places where there are no plants or animals.

Bacteria commonly cause infections that affect the lungs such as tuberculosis but they can also cause diseases such as tetanus, typhoid and blood poisoning.

The Black Death, a bubonic plague that wiped out millions of people in Europe in the 1340s, was a bacteria.

VIRUSES

Viruses are similar to bacteria in the sense that they are simple and very small. However viruses are seen as an infectious agent and not a living organism. Some scientists even call them a type of parasite as they can only replicate inside the living cells of an organism. Viruses can infect all types of organisms, from animals and plants to bacteria.

Every virus has a small piece of DNA or RNA (not both) that is the core of the virus. Surrounding this is a protein coat for protection called a capsid. The capsid is also the part of the virus used to infect other organisms. Viruses need to infect or invade a host cell in order to reproduce as they cannot do this on their own. Viruses are seen as non-living as they do not respond to anything. If you try to do something to them they either continue to function or are destroyed. They also do not have any working parts. While there are some advanced viruses that seem complex, viruses do not have any of the parts you would normally think of when you think of a cell. They have no nuclei, mitochondria, or ribosomes. Some viruses do not even have cytoplasm.

VIRUS FACTS

Millions of viruses can fit inside a single cell. Viruses are the smallest living organisms in the world!

Diseases such as colds, flu, measles and chickenpox are all caused by viruses.

An epidemic occurs if more people than usual catch a viral infection. A pandemic is an epidemic that affects people worldwide.
In 1918 the flu virus infected a third of the world's population and approximately 50 million people died.

DID YOU KNOW?

The word virus is from the Latin virus referring to poison and other noxious substances, first used in English in 1392.

Like bacteria there are three basic shapes of a virus

Helical virions are set up like a tube. The protein coat winds up like a garden hose around the core.

There is the polyhedral shape. This shape group includes the classic virus shape that looks like a dodecahedron. A dodecahedron is a geometric shape with twelve sides. These viruses have many facets and a seemingly hard shell of capsomeres (pieces of a capsid).

There are also complex virus shapes with a geometric head and long legs.

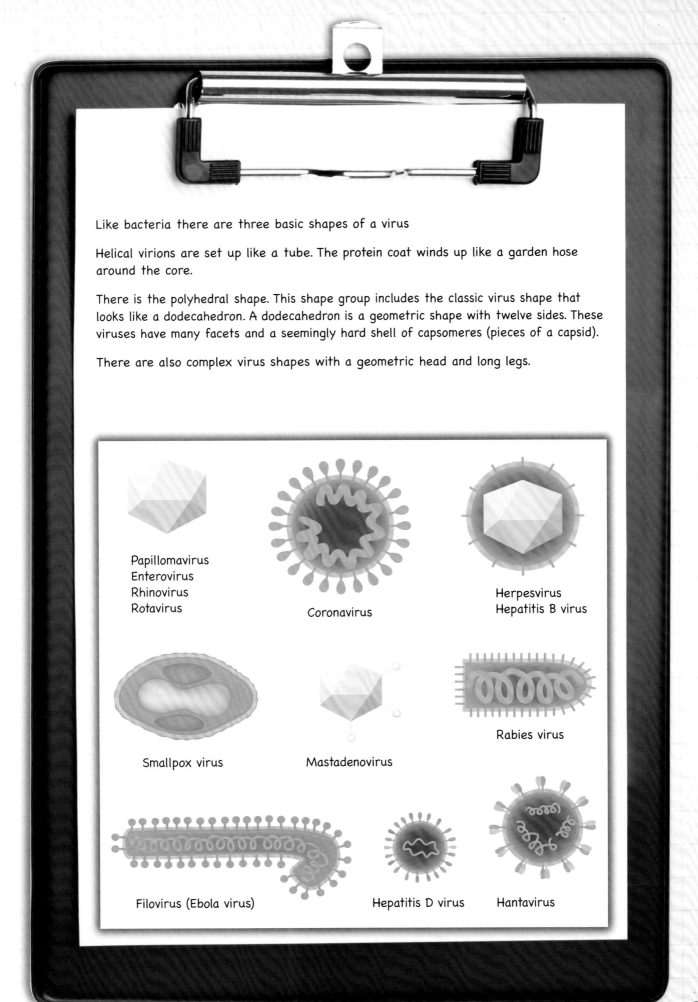

Papillomavirus
Enterovirus
Rhinovirus
Rotavirus

Coronavirus

Herpesvirus
Hepatitis B virus

Smallpox virus

Mastadenovirus

Rabies virus

Filovirus (Ebola virus)

Hepatitis D virus

Hantavirus

WHAT MAKES US HUMAN?

We are a species of animal and share many physical characteristics with lots of creatures. Humans contain 96-98% of the same DNA as chimpanzees or gorillas, yet we are also very different. So what makes us special and what makes us human? There are many special aspects that make us separate from the animal kingdom.

Humor – There is no other creature able to appreciate, create and express humor.

Appreciation of beauty – Humans are the only animal to be able to appreciate all kinds of beauty, such as a sunset, a work of art, an intricate design. Of course, many birds are attracted to a mating partner's showy plumage.

Self-consciousness – Except for a few animals that can recognize themselves, humans are the only ones who have the ability to be a spectator, critic or admirer of the world around them. Humans can analyze and understand the causes and consequences of their actions.

Awareness of death – Animals might have a survival instinct, but we humans are able to consider that one day we will die and we have a deep respect for mortality. All cultures across the globe perform some sort of funeral ceremony when a person dies.

Understanding time - Animals have time instinct which is usually influenced by environmental changes or subconscious bodily processes managed by DNA and hormonal release. We are the only animal that can think about history, the future and understand time, which is after all a human invention.

201

Complex communication - Many animals can understand simple words or tones but they do not communicate in complex sentences. Human beings have created hundreds of languages, even though they are born without any way to communicate.

Meaning of life – As humans, we often wonder what the purpose of our existence is. What is life's meaning? No other animal contemplates its reason for living and they would also not be willing to die for specific values or beliefs.

Adaptability - We are able to adapt to our surroundings in extremes better than all other animals, perhaps even better than plant life. We wear clothes, build shelters, exist in every corner of Earth and have even ventured into space.

A sense of morality – Animals do not have an understanding of right and wrong. Some suggest that this is because humans created the idea of what is right or wrong and that this one aspect is what significantly separates us from the animal kingdom. The ability to know right from wrong and to change from doing something wrong to doing something right, even when there are pressures and temptations, is called character. This is only found in human beings.

Angels

Devils

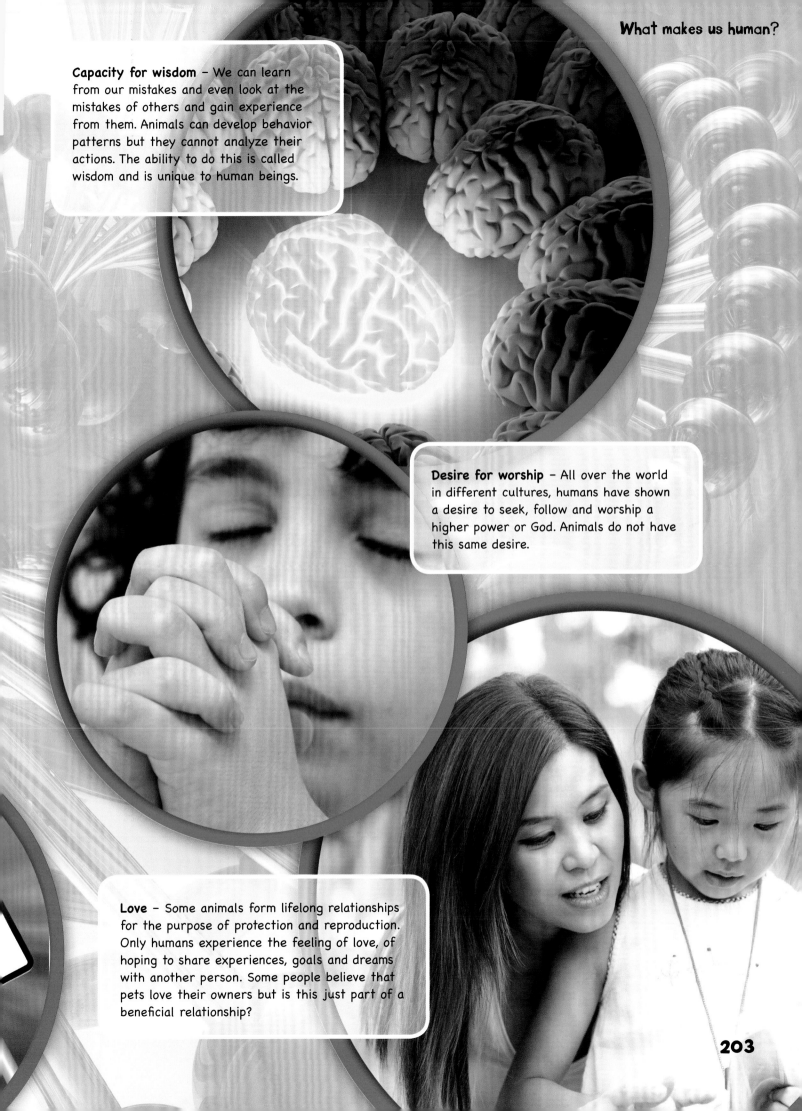

Capacity for wisdom – We can learn from our mistakes and even look at the mistakes of others and gain experience from them. Animals can develop behavior patterns but they cannot analyze their actions. The ability to do this is called wisdom and is unique to human beings.

Desire for worship – All over the world in different cultures, humans have shown a desire to seek, follow and worship a higher power or God. Animals do not have this same desire.

Love – Some animals form lifelong relationships for the purpose of protection and reproduction. Only humans experience the feeling of love, of hoping to share experiences, goals and dreams with another person. Some people believe that pets love their owners but is this just part of a beneficial relationship?

203

COMMUNICATION

Many animals communicate and not always just by sound. Humans are no different and as social animals, we need to communicate. We use communication as a way of protecting ourselves, for example we shout for help if we are in danger. We need to communicate to learn basic human practices, but also to share new things that we have learned with others. We also use communication to form relationships with each other, to express love, to demonstrate anger and cover the whole range of emotions we feel throughout our lifetimes.

Interpersonal communication, which is communicating with other people, does not necessarily mean speaking, or even making a noise. The way you shrug your shoulders to say 'I don't know' or the way you frown at something that you do not approve of are both forms of communication. Even more subtle forms of communication are used each day, a glance helps others know that you are there and which direction you are walking when in a busy street, a gaze or averted look may indicate intimacy, submission or dominance.

DID YOU KNOW?

Most communication is in fact how we move our body, or our body language. The least part of communicating is actually language, so what you say does not really matter, it's how you say it.

LANGUAGE

Language is a unique human invention. No other animal uses language to communicate, but it is an ability that none of us are born with. We all have to learn language and it takes years, sometimes even a lifetime, to master. To begin with, we learn language the way we learn many other skills, simply by copying and by trial and error. Language is the result of social interaction. If there were no others around us to correct us or teach us, we would not learn to speak at all. In each language, there is a complex set of rules to follow and, although these rules form the foundation of the language, the languages are evolving and changing all the time. There are an estimated 6,000 to 7,000 languages in the world, although many of these may be called dialects. A dialect is an evolution of another language which has similarities to its original language but can result in many different words and phrases. What is even more interesting is that language has developed from simple speech into the written word and even sign language and Braille. Sign language was developed in order to help deaf people communicate and Braille was developed to help blind people communicate.

Language is thought to have originated when early humans started to change the way they communicated with each other and began to acquire the ability to understand the thoughts of others and share their experiences. This development happened at the same time as an increase in brain volume, which in turn was perhaps a result of an increased ability to work together to hunt food and protect the young from predators.

Languages evolve and change over time and many have become extinct or developed into new modern languages. The languages which are most spoken in the world today belong to:

the **Indo-European** languages, which include languages such as English, Spanish, Portuguese, Russian, and Hindi.

the **Sino-Tibetan** languages, which include Mandarin Chinese, Cantonese, and many others.

the **Afro-Asiatic** languages, which include Arabic, Amharic, Somali, and Hebrew.

the **Bantu** languages, which include Swahili, Zulu, Shona, and hundreds of other languages spoken throughout Africa.

LANGUAGE LOSS

Many people believe that with the advance of global communication, between 70%–90% of the languages we speak today will become extinct by the year 2100.

AMAZING LANGUAGE

Language is also a way for us to communicate our artistic abilities and express our feelings. Think of all the famous writers through the ages who have used language to communicate their talent and helped us to appreciate the beauty of words or understand more about how we think.

CONFUCIUS

VOLTAIRE

SHAKESPEARE

WORDSWORTH

PLATO

SCOTT FITZGERALD

HEMINGWAY

207

FACTS AND MYTHS OF THE HUMAN BODY

FUNKY FACTS!

Every atom of our body is said to be billions of years old.

Our body is 70% water.

On average, we produce around 10,000 gallons of saliva over the course of our lifetime.

You cannot breathe and swallow at the same time, unless you are a baby who can do this until they are 9 months old

The average human body sheds around 40 pounds of skin over a lifetime.

It is impossible to sneeze without blinking your eyes.

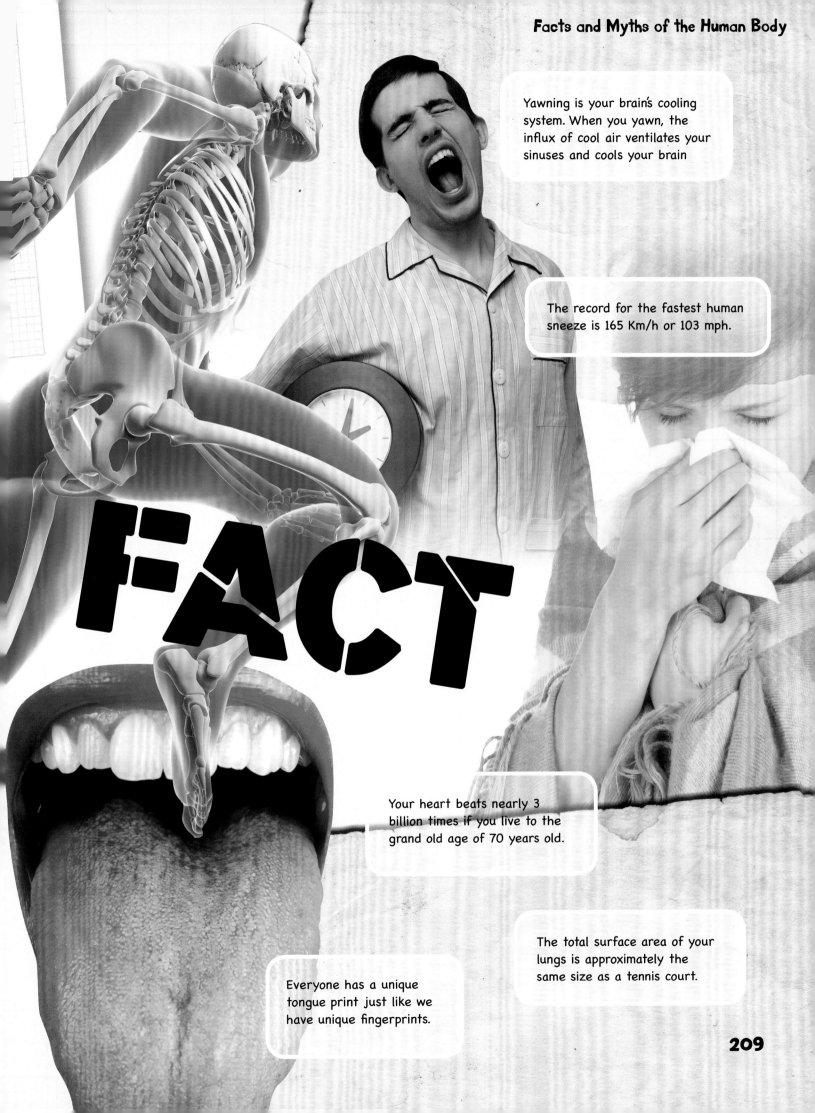

Yawning is your brain's cooling system. When you yawn, the influx of cool air ventilates your sinuses and cools your brain

The record for the fastest human sneeze is 165 Km/h or 103 mph.

FACT

Your heart beats nearly 3 billion times if you live to the grand old age of 70 years old.

The total surface area of your lungs is approximately the same size as a tennis court.

Everyone has a unique tongue print just like we have unique fingerprints.

209

MYSTERIOUS MYTHS

Eating sugar makes children hyperactive.
Children of the world unite, educate your parents that they are not telling the truth! Scientific experiments have concluded that there is absolutely no connection between a child's behavior and their sugar intake.

Missing out meals helps you lose weight.
This is most definitely not true. If you miss one meal, you will overeat the next, but more importantly eating a regular meal keeps your metabolic rate up. If you miss a meal, your body does not know when it is going to get fuel next so it goes into starvation mode. This means that the next thing you eat is partially stored as fat for the future when you may not get any food.

Knuckle cracking will cause arthritis.
This is not true, although if you are a persistent cracker then it can weaken joints. Arthritis is a disease of the bones and the cracking in your knuckles has nothing to do with your bones, it is the sound of small bubbles of gas bursting.

You lose most of your body heat through your head.
Obviously if your head is the only exposed part of your body while everything is wrapped up in clothes, then you will lose most heat from the head. However, when it is unclothed your body will lose heat from all over. It has been proven that you lose around 10% of the heat from your head, not most of it.

Sleepwalkers should never be woken.
In fact, it is much better to wake a sleepwalker as they may injure themselves from tripping over things or walking into dangerous zones, even if they wake up confused and disoriented.

Hair products can cure split ends.
Nope, sorry, there is no evidence supporting this, although some shampoos and conditioners might help prevent them. The only cure for split ends is to cut them.

Reading in the dark will ruin your eyesight. Sorry but yet another false fact parents tell their children. Although it is true that dimmer light makes your eyes work a little harder, it does not mean that it is damaging to your eyes.

Different areas of the tongue taste different things. This myth has been around for decades and is the result of a tongue map that was mistranslated by a Harvard professor from a badly written and discredited German paper. In fact, every area of the tongue can taste every type of flavour, which are: sweet, sour, savory salty and bitter.

Fingernails and hair continue to grow after death. This is just not true. Neither your fingernails nor your hair continues to grow. What happens is that the skin and cuticles shrink after death, making it look as though the hair and nails have grown.

You can be double jointed. No one yet has ever been born with truly double joints. Some people can have unusual joints where the fibrous tissues joining the bones together are more elastic or flexible than normal. This can arise from constant practice and exercise, such as contortionists do, or it can be hereditary.

BUSTER

You will catch a cold if you go out in cold, wet weather. In fact there is no evidence to support this at all. The cold virus is perhaps more common as a result of more people spending time indoors in close proximity to one another.

Shaved hair grows back thicker and darker. Uncut hair has more exposure to the sun which may lighten it, so regrown hair may appear comparatively darker.

You can catch warts from touching a toad. Completely bogus fact! The bumps on a toad are not warts but glands. The papilloma virus causes warts and it only affects humans.

211

GLOSSARY

Abdomen Part of the body between the chest and hip bone containing the stomach and major organs.

Acids Substance that helps in the breakdown of food for the digestive process.

Alveoli Tiny sacs in the lungs where the exchange of oxygen and carbon dioxide takes place.

Arteries Tubes that form a branching system and carry blood away from the heart to the cells, tissues, and organs of the body.

Biceps Large muscle in the front of the upper arm that flexes the forearm.

Bile A fluid that is secreted by the liver and stored in the gallbladder, used in digestion and absorption of fat.

Bladder Stretchy bag with muscular wall that collects and stores urine.

Bloodstream The flow of blood around the body.

Body Regions Anatomical areas of the body.

Bone marrow Substance in the middle of a bone that produces blood cells for the body.

Bronchi Main branches of the trachea that lead directly to the lungs.

Capillaries Tiny blood vessels that connect arteries and veins, where the exchange of carbon dioxide and oxygen take place.

Carbon dioxide Gas formed during respiration.

Cardiovascular Relating to the heart and blood vessels (also known as the circulatory system).

Cartilage Strong but flexible material found in areas of the body including the ears, nose, knees and joints.

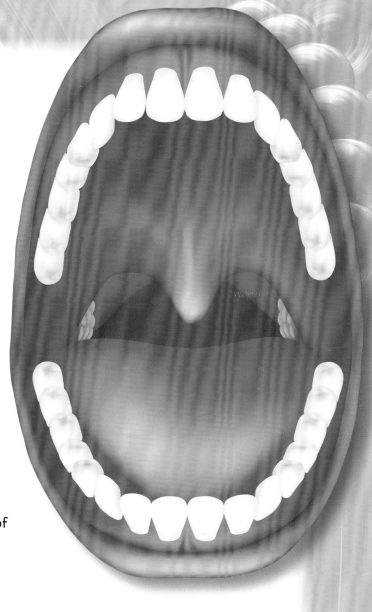

Cavity A hole, or hollow space.

Cell The smallest unit of life – all living things are made up of cells.

Clavicle Bone linking the scapula and sternum also known as the collar bone.

Corneas Transparent outer coat of the eyeball.

Digestive System A group of organs stretching from the mouth to the anus, serving to break down foods, gather nutrients, and expel waste.

Diaphragm Muscle that separates the abdominal and thoracic cavities and helps in breathing.

DNA A chemical in every cell that controls the cell's shape, purpose and the way it behaves.

Epiglottis A flap of tissue at the bottom of the tongue that stops food going into the trachea.

Embryo An animal or plant in its earliest stage of development.

Enzyme Chemical that helps to break down and digest food.

Esophagus Muscular tube for the passage of food from the pharynx to the stomach.

Exhale Breathing out and discharging air.

External On the outside of the body.

Fallopian tubes Two tubes that connect the ovaries to the womb in females.

Femur Bone that extends from the pelvis to the knee. The longest and thickest bone in the human body.

Fibula The outer and thinner of the two bones of the leg found between the knee and ankle.

Germ A tiny, single-cell, life-form that often spreads disease.

Gland An organ that makes a particular chemical, or substance to be released inside, or outside the body. Hormones and sweat are made by glands.

Hepatic Relating to the liver.

Humerus Long bone of the arm, extending from the shoulder to the elbow.

Immune Protected against, or not at risk from, a particular type of germ, or disease, such as measles.

Infection A disease caused by a germ that gets inside the body and begins to multiply.

Inhale Filling the lungs with fresh, oxygen-rich air.

Internal On the inside of the body.

Involuntary An action that takes place without us choosing, or deciding to do it.

Joint The area where two bones are attached for the purpose of permitting body parts to move.

Keratin A tough, chemical substance and the main element in our hair and nails.

Kidney Organ used to maintain water and electrolyte balance along with filtering the blood of waste products.

Larynx Part of the respiratory tract in the throat area that contains the vocal cords.

Ligament A band of tissue, usually white and fibrous which connects bones, cartilages or supporting muscles or organs.

Lungs Respiratory organs in the chest cavity that together with the heart work to remove carbon dioxide from the blood and provide it with oxygen.

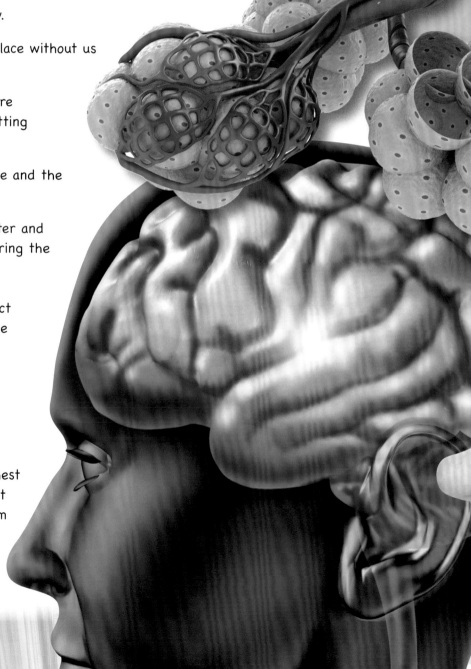

Membrane Thin, pliable layer of tissue that covers surfaces or separates or connects other body parts.

Melanin A pigment found in hair, skin and eyes.

Metacarpus Part of hand that includes the five bones between the fingers and the wrist.

Muscle A tissue composed of fibers capable of contracting to allow body movement.

Nasal cavity The air passage behind the nose from which moisture is added to the air you breathe during the breathing process.

Nervous System A network of specialized cells that communicate information about the body's surroundings and itself.

Nephrons Filtering units of the kidney that remove waste matter from the blood

Nucleus The part of a cell that controls the rest of the cell.

Nutrients Chemicals, often obtained from food, that a plant or animal needs in order to live and grow.

Olfactory Relating to smells or the sense of smell.

Organ A part of the body that has a particular job to do.

Ovary A female reproductive organ that produces eggs and female sex hormones.

Oxygen An element essential for respiration, essential to life.

Particle A tiny piece of matter or substance.

Pancreas Long, irregularly shaped gland that produces enzymes and hormones that aid digestion.

Patella A small flat triangular bone in front of the knee that protects the knee joint.

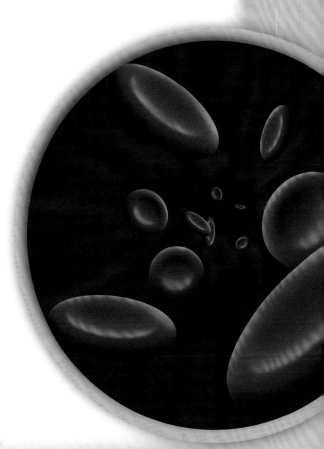

Pelvis The structure of the skeleton that supports the lower limbs.

Peristalsis Wavelike muscular contractions that help to move food down the digestive system.

Pharynx Section that extends from the mouth and nasal cavities to the larynx.

Pigment A substance that makes or gives something a particular hue such as green or blue.

Process A series of actions, changes, or functions bringing about a result.

Respiration A process by which the body's cells use oxygen in order to break down nutrients and supply the body with energy.

Rib cage Enclosing structure formed by the ribs and the bones to which they are attached, that forms a cage to protect the heart and lungs.

Saliva A watery substance made in the mouth, also known as spit.

Sensory Linked to the senses, sight, hearing, smell, taste and touch.

Skeletal Relating to the skeleton or bones of the skeleton.

Tarsal One of the seven bones in the ankle.

Tendons A band of tough fibrous tissue that connects a muscle to a bone.

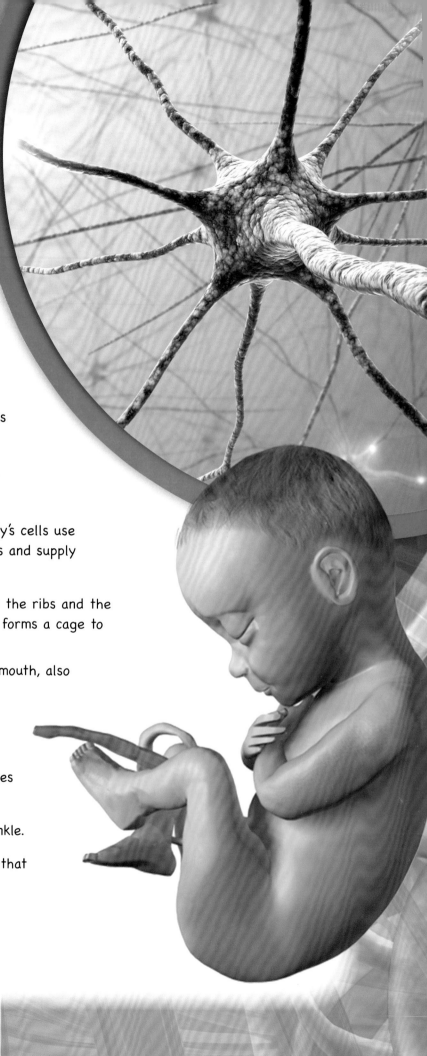

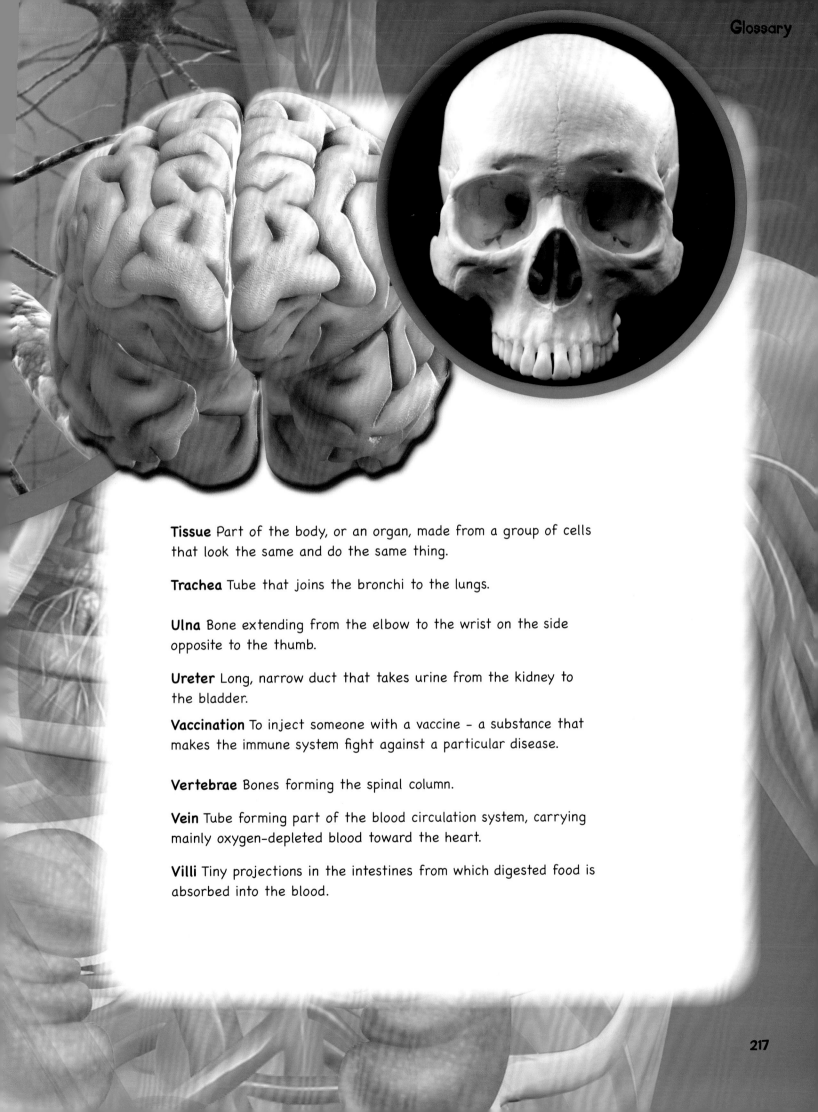

Tissue Part of the body, or an organ, made from a group of cells that look the same and do the same thing.

Trachea Tube that joins the bronchi to the lungs.

Ulna Bone extending from the elbow to the wrist on the side opposite to the thumb.

Ureter Long, narrow duct that takes urine from the kidney to the bladder.

Vaccination To inject someone with a vaccine - a substance that makes the immune system fight against a particular disease.

Vertebrae Bones forming the spinal column.

Vein Tube forming part of the blood circulation system, carrying mainly oxygen-depleted blood toward the heart.

Villi Tiny projections in the intestines from which digested food is absorbed into the blood.

INDEX

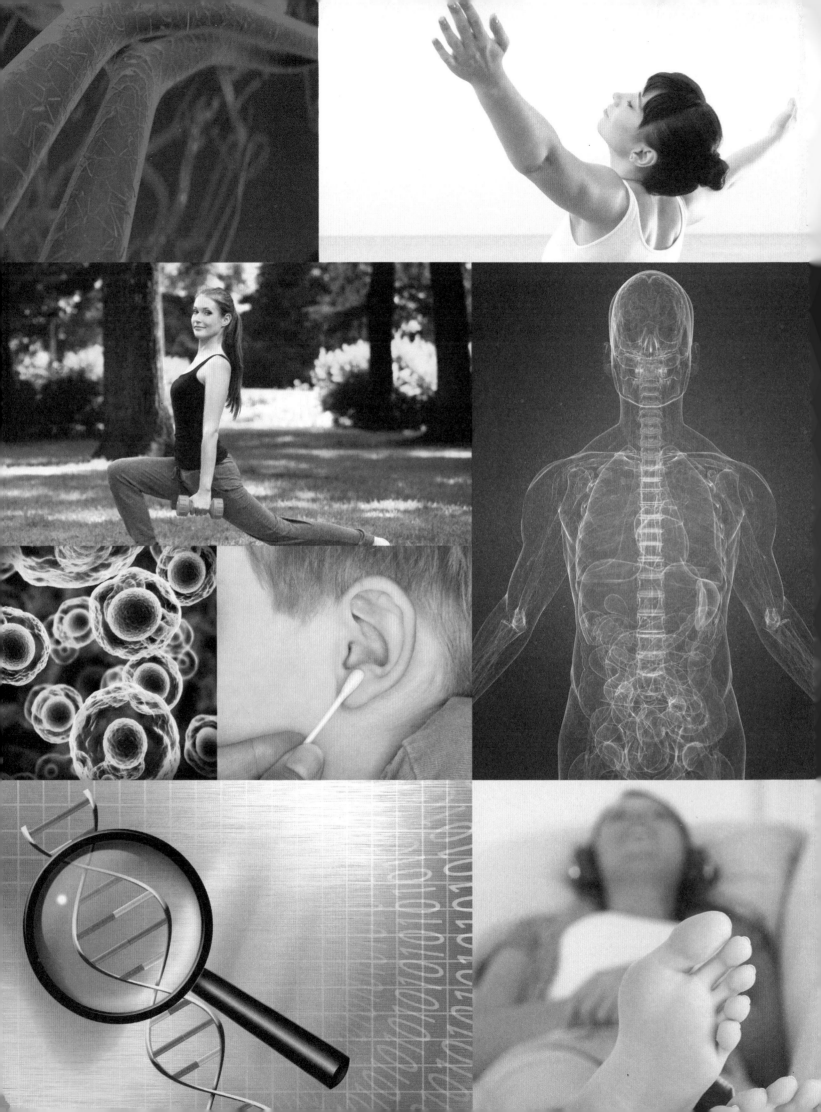